Y0-CLE-750

SEE AND SEW

# see and sew

## A PICTURE BOOK OF SEWING

by mariska karasz

DRAWINGS BY CHRISTINE ENGLER

PHILADELPHIA • J. B. LIPPINCOTT COMPANY • NEW YORK

Sixth Impression

Printed in the United States of America

To my little sewing class of last summer:

Solveig, Rozsika, Carola, Barbara, Ilonka.

And to

all the little girls who want to learn to sew.

# ACKNOWLEDGMENT

The author wishes to thank the principals and sewing teachers of the following schools for their cooperation:

Lincoln School of Teachers College, New York City, N. Y.

Birch Wathen School, New York City, N. Y.

Walt Whitman School, New York City, N. Y.

Manumit School, Pawling, N. Y.

Public School 93, New York City, N. Y.

P. S. 132, Springfield Gardens, Queens, N. Y.

Manhattan Trade School for Girls, New York City, N. Y.

Milltown District School, Brewster, N. Y.

# FIND THE RIGHT PAGE HERE

## AUTHOR'S FOREWORD

My eyes were fastened on the needle of the seamstress who came to make our clothes every year. Finally I could hold my question no longer. "Miss Margit . . ."

Her eyes turned from her work to my face. "Yes, child."

"How do you put so many stitches on your needle?"

Her eyes smiled and she answered: "When I was seven, I couldn't do it either. But you're never too young to learn."

That was all I needed. I retreated to a corner of the sofa with a threaded needle and some cloth. Half an hour later my little piece of cloth was much the worse for wear and the thread was very dirty, but I had accomplished nothing. Besides, my palm hurt, because I had used it to push the needle through the cloth. In despair I looked up at Miss Margit . . . only to find that she was looking at me and smiling broadly.

"But, child! You must use a little magic in all sewing! See this thimble?"

And that was indeed the first time I had ever noticed it. I have never been without it since. On that very afternoon she helped me to make a little apron. Every stitch was my own and I loved it.

Now I am trying, in this book, to give you this same Magic of the Thimble.

# LEARN A SECRET ABOUT MATERIAL

Find a small scrap of cloth. The size of your hand is enough. It may be any shape, but without pattern. Look at it closely. Hold it up and see it through the light. You will see the threads crossing each other.

Stretch along the threads going in one direction. Turn the material and stretch it along the threads going in the other direction.
Do you feel the difference? If you do, you have the clue to a Secret.

# WARP AND WOOF

In weaving, the first threads laid lengthwise on the loom are called the warp. In dressmaking this is called the lengthwise grain. These threads are stronger because they have to bear all the weight of the other threads crossing them. The warp usually stretches less when you test your material to feel the difference.

The thread that is woven under and over from edge to edge is called the woof, or filling yarn. In dressmaking this is called the cross-wise grain or the crosswise of the goods.

The loops made by the turning of the thread at the edges are called the selvedge or self-edge. The selvedge goes along the warp thread, which always runs along the length of cloth.

# THE A.B.C. OF DRESSMAKING

Knowing how to cut your pattern on the cloth is the A.B.C. of dressmaking.

A. In weaving, we say the thread; in dressmaking it's the grain of the material.

B. In weaving, we say the warp, or up and down threads; while in dressmaking it is called the lengthwise of the goods.

C. The woof or filler of weaving is the crosswise of the goods in sewing.

In cutting a dress you must know which parts of the dress are cut lengthwise, and which on the crosswise grain. So first you must be able to recognize the lengthwise and crosswise of your fabric. See if you can tell which is the lengthwise grain of your own dress, without the aid of the selvedge.

Another clue: The warp thread may look a little coarser and straighter than the woof threads, which are usually softer and more wiggly. You can see if this is true by fraying the top and side of a scrap of cloth. Break the threads you pull out. Which ones are easier to break?

One more hint: In washing, material will shrink more lengthwise because the warp threads are pulled tighter in weaving to support the weight of the woof.

Perhaps at first you won't be able to tell the difference between the warp and the woof—that is, the lengthwise and crosswise of every piece of material you pick up—but with practice, you can become a wizard at it.

# WHAT FABRICS ARE MADE OF

When you pick up a piece of material, see if you can tell what it is made of. All materials can be classified according to the fibre or fibres from which they are woven.

## I. PLANT FIBRES

Cotton 

batiste
calico
cheesecloth
crash
denim
flannelette
gingham
jersey
lawn
percale
piqué
seersucker

Flax

crash linen
damask
dress linen
handkerchief linen
huck linen
table linen

## II. ANIMAL FIBRES

Silk

brocade
chiffon
china silk
crepe
satin
taffeta

Wool

challis
flannel
jersey
homespun
serge
tweed

## III. MANUFACTURED OR SYNTHETIC FIBRES

Rayon

Nylon

Aralac 

# GET ACQUAINTED WITH YOUR TAPE MEASURE

1". This is an inch.

3/4". This is three-quarters of an inch.

1/4". This is a quarter of an inch.

1/2". This is a half-inch, the size of a basting stitch.

1/8". This is one-eighth of an inch, size of a running stitch.

3/8". This is three-eighths of an inch.

A yard is 36 inches. A half-yard is 18 inches. A quarter of a yard is 9 inches. What is 27 inches?

There are two sides to every tape measure. Always start measuring from number one at either end, and do not twist the tape.

# THE DIFFERENCE BETWEEN SCISSORS

Scissors have both handles equal size. They may be larger than shears but if the handles are the same size they are called scissors. There are three kinds of scissors.

1. The Blunt with neither tip pointed. Perhaps you used them when you were very young.

2. The Medium either with one tip pointed. These are used for all kinds of sewing.

3. Or with both tips pointed.

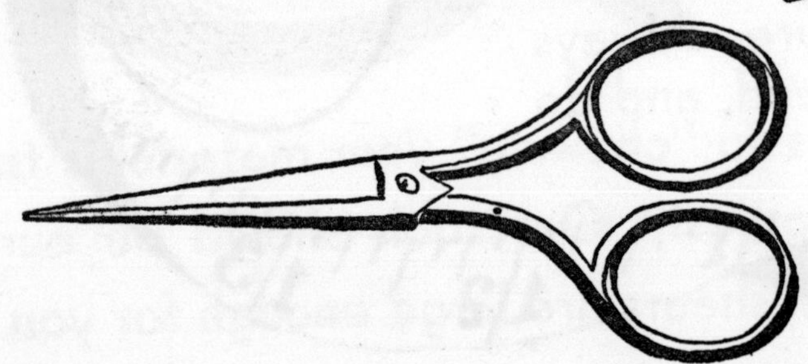

These are good for snipping threads, for ripping, or for cutting threads in embroidery.

## . . . AND SHEARS

Shears have one handle (called bow handle) larger than the other, so that on one side four fingers may be used in holding them. Their weight is a help in cutting.

Dressmakers use shears with the bent handle. They won't pull your material off the table and give that "chewed off" look.

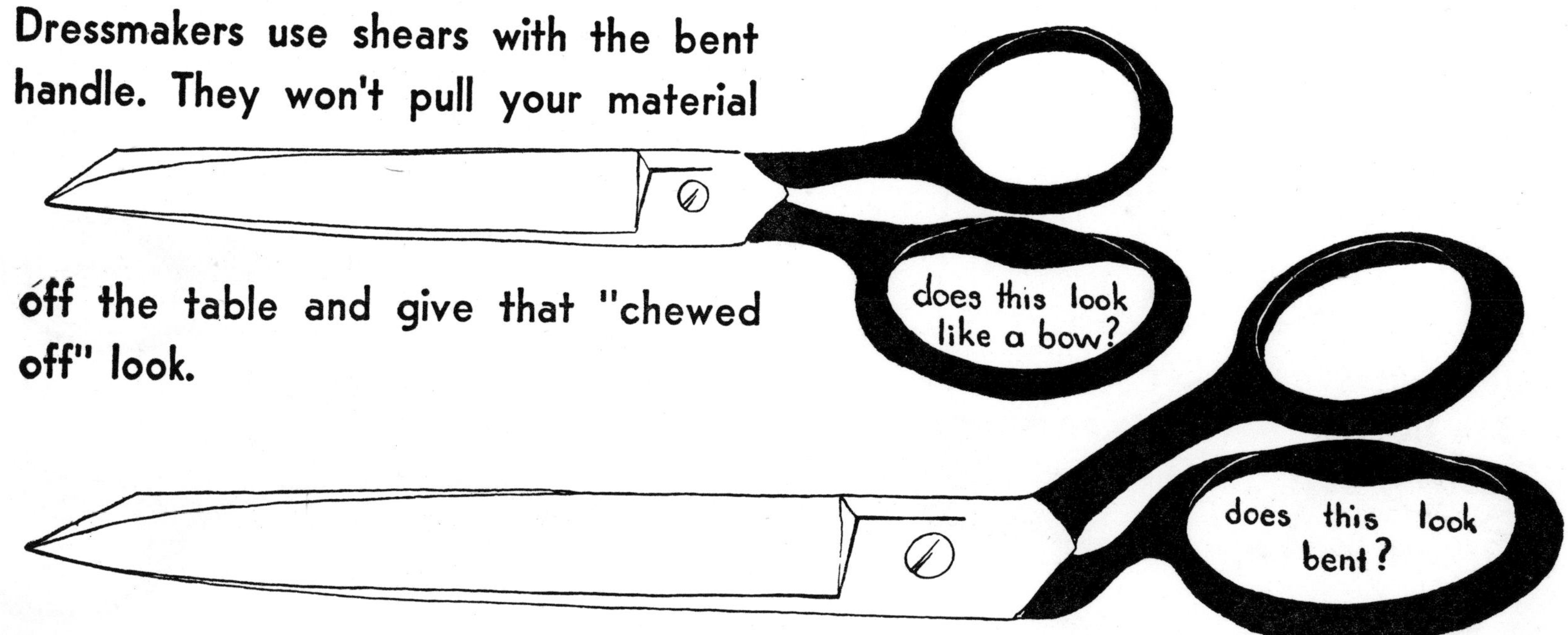


The quickest way to get a pair of scissors or shears to "chewing" your material is to cut anything but cloth with it (paper, string, apples!). Our tools should be our servants, the right size for the right job. Seven-inch shears are large enough for you.

But scissors can't cut wood.

How to cut the stuffing out of a sofa . . .

# WHAT WOULD YOU LIKE TO MAKE FIRST?

Does your mother need a small tray cloth . . . or your doll a bedspread?

You can make both of these out of half a yard of material. A deep bright shade of cotton crash or plain gingham will take chalk marks for your design. Any white or light material will have to be marked with pencil, which spoils the looks of your work till after washing. Linen wears, irons and frays well, comes in good colors, but is many times more expensive than cotton.

# DRAWING A THREAD

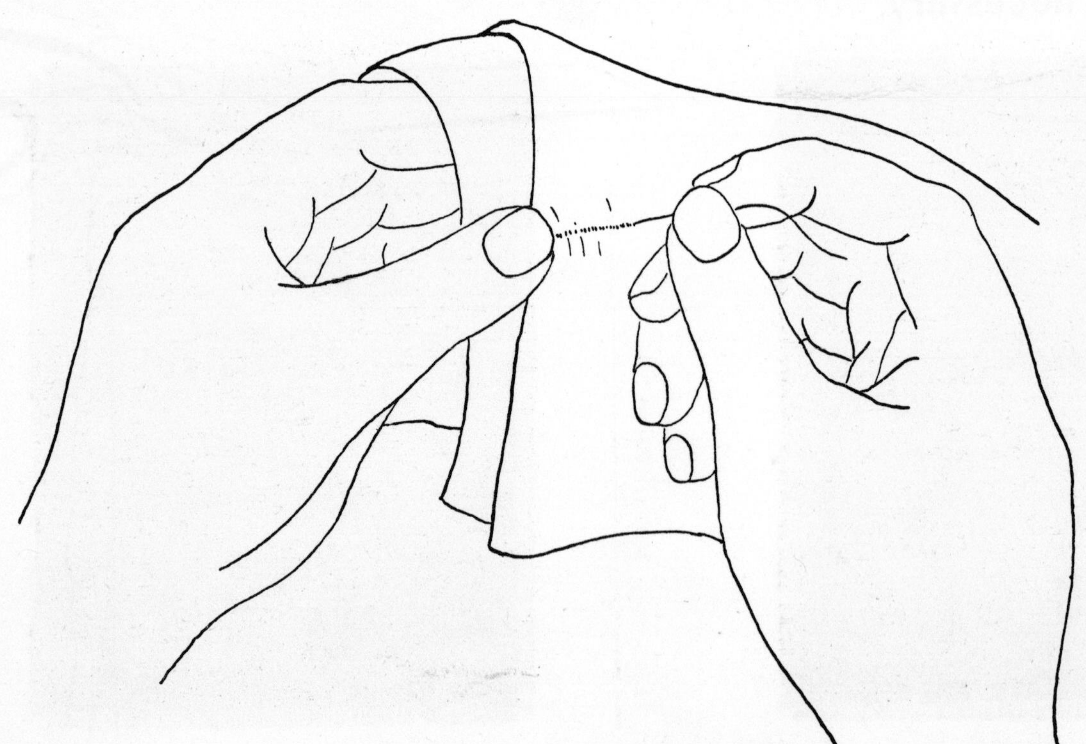

Drawing a thread of the material is an aid to cutting it straight. With a pin's point and your sharp little eyes, pull up a thread along which you want to cut. Draw it out, even if it breaks often. Sometimes just starting this way will get your eyes used to cutting even with the thread of the goods.

## CUTTING YOUR TRAY CLOTH AND DOLL'S BEDSPREAD

**If your material is uneven, cut the four edges straight. Draw a thread if necessary.**

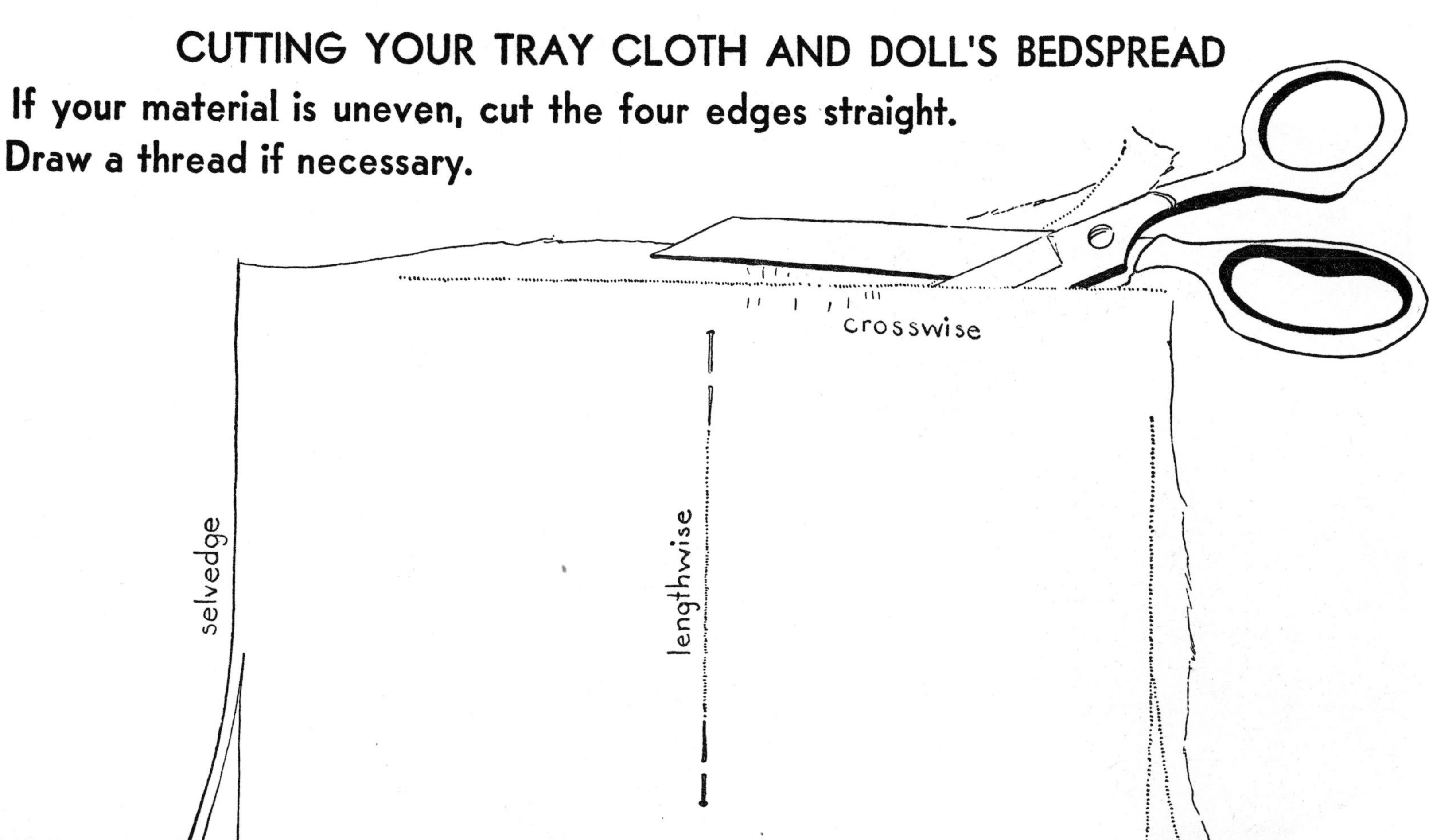


**Fold your evenly-cut piece of cloth in half by putting the two short edges together. Mark center with two pins and draw a thread between them. Cut in half. One is the doll's bedspread. Fringe it all around a half inch deep.**

# HOW TO HOLD SHEARS

Never shut your eyes at a point like this.

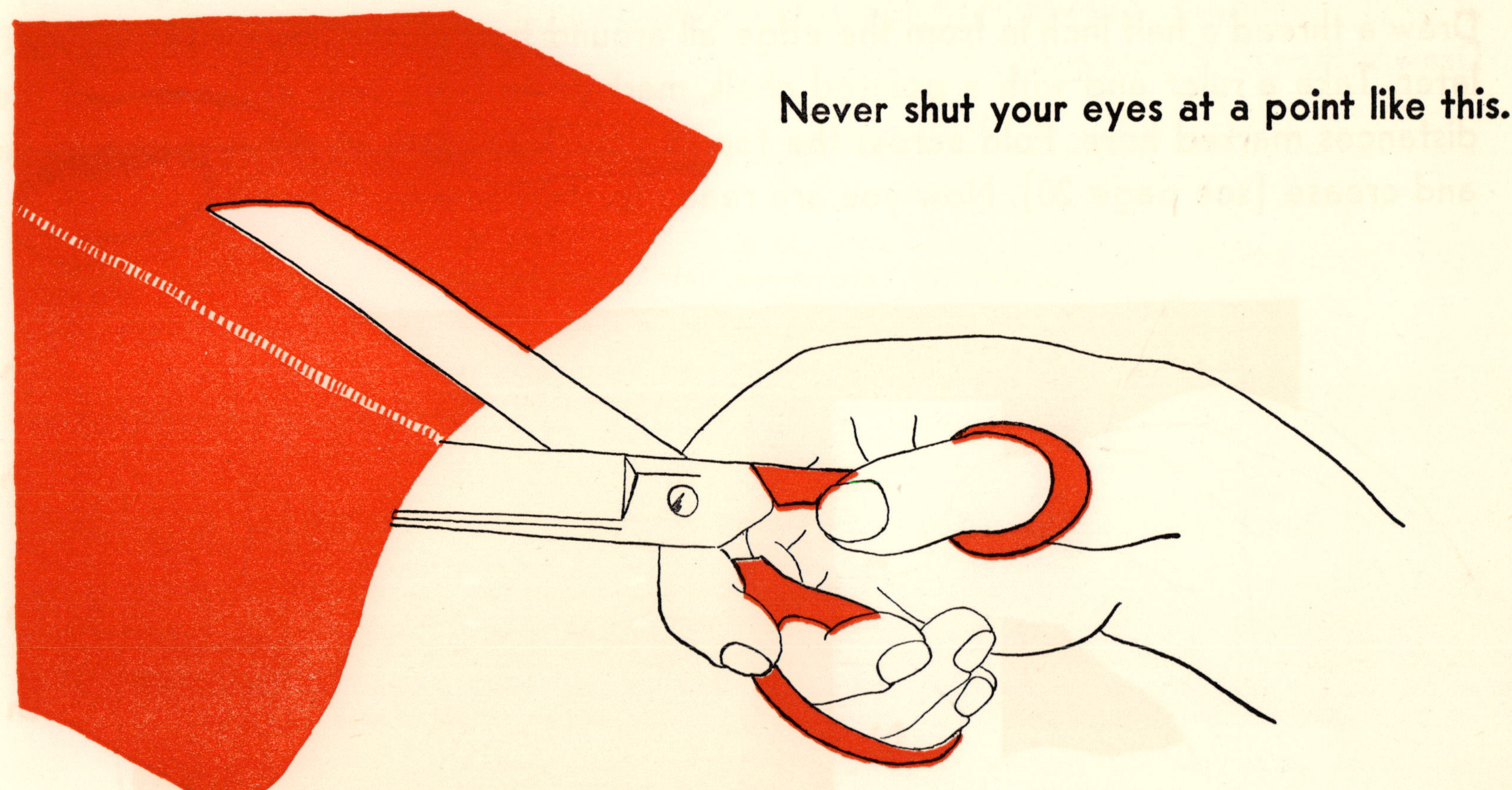

Hold shears with three fingers in large handle, thumb in the other, forefinger holding the outside of bow handle.
Keep pointed blade down; it goes under the cloth better.

# MARKING YOUR TRAY CLOTH FOR DECORATION

Draw a thread a half inch in from the edge all around tray cloth. This is for fringing it later. Take a ruler and with a pointed chalk, mark down from your drawn thread the distances marked here. Fold across the top of your tray cloth at the first inch-marks and crease (see page 20). Now you are ready to start sewing.

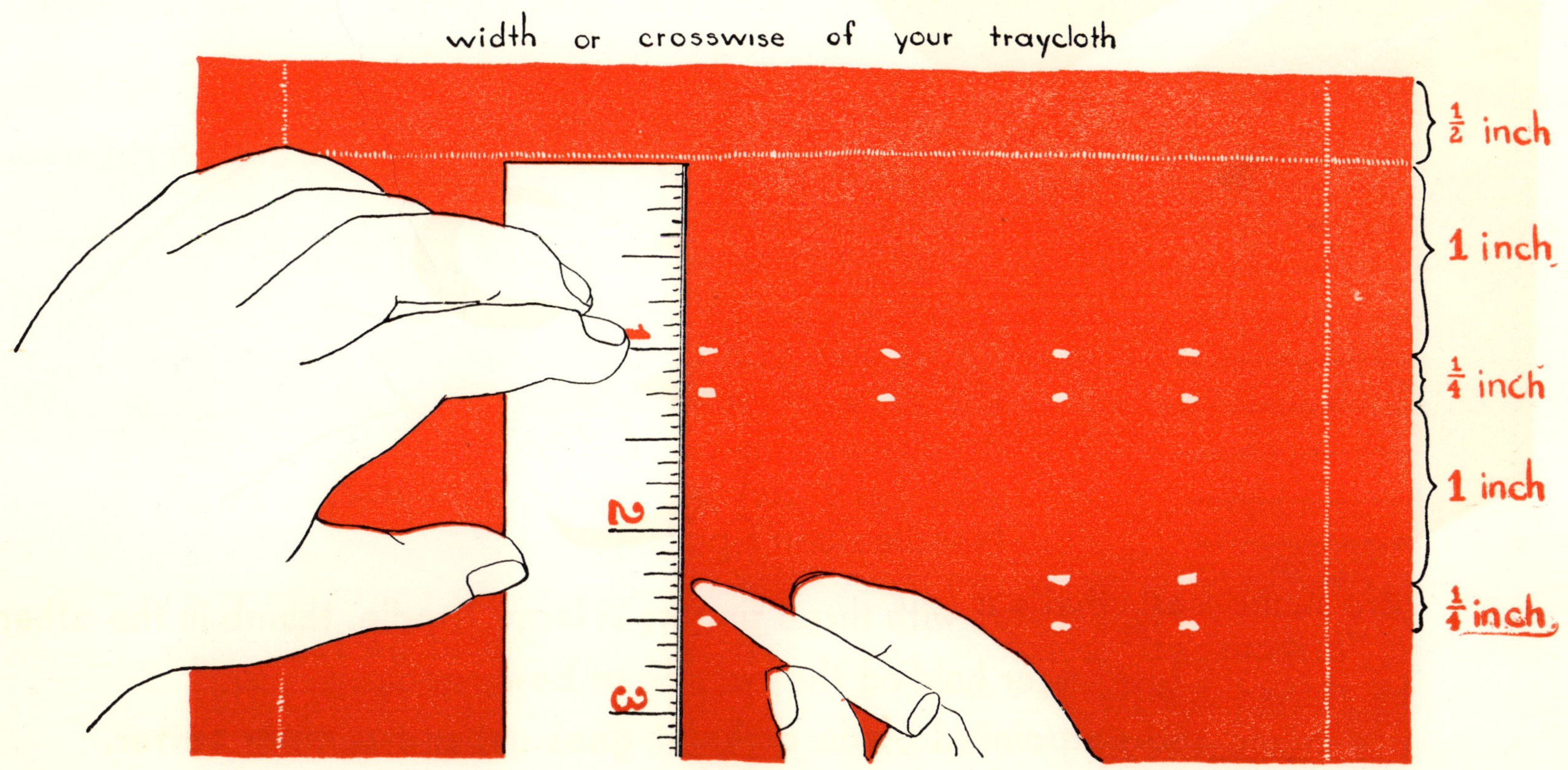

# CHOOSING YOUR NEEDLE

There are three kinds of needles: crewels, darners and sharps. Crewels are short needles with long eyes. Darners are long needles with long eyes. Sharps are short with small eyes. Short needles are the best for you.

For embroidery there is a long-eyed thick needle, with a point. Also there are tapestry needles with large eyes and blunt points. These are good for loosely woven fabrics, such as you would use for cross-stitch.

For ordinary sewing try to remember these little rhymes:

3
4
5
6
7
8
9
10

Needles go from 3 to 10
You must know which to use and when.
Don't use needles much too big
You should see the holes they dig.
Use a needle number nine
If your cloth is rather fine
And don't pick a thread too coarse,
Needles can't pull like a horse.

Threads are numbered, that's a fact
For color, "mercerized" select.
Match the thread a little darker . . .
You want a seam, and not a marker.

Should you want your thread to show
Its number should be rather low.
For basting this is really nifty.
For all the rest use number fifty.

# THREADING THE NEEDLE

Lean one hand

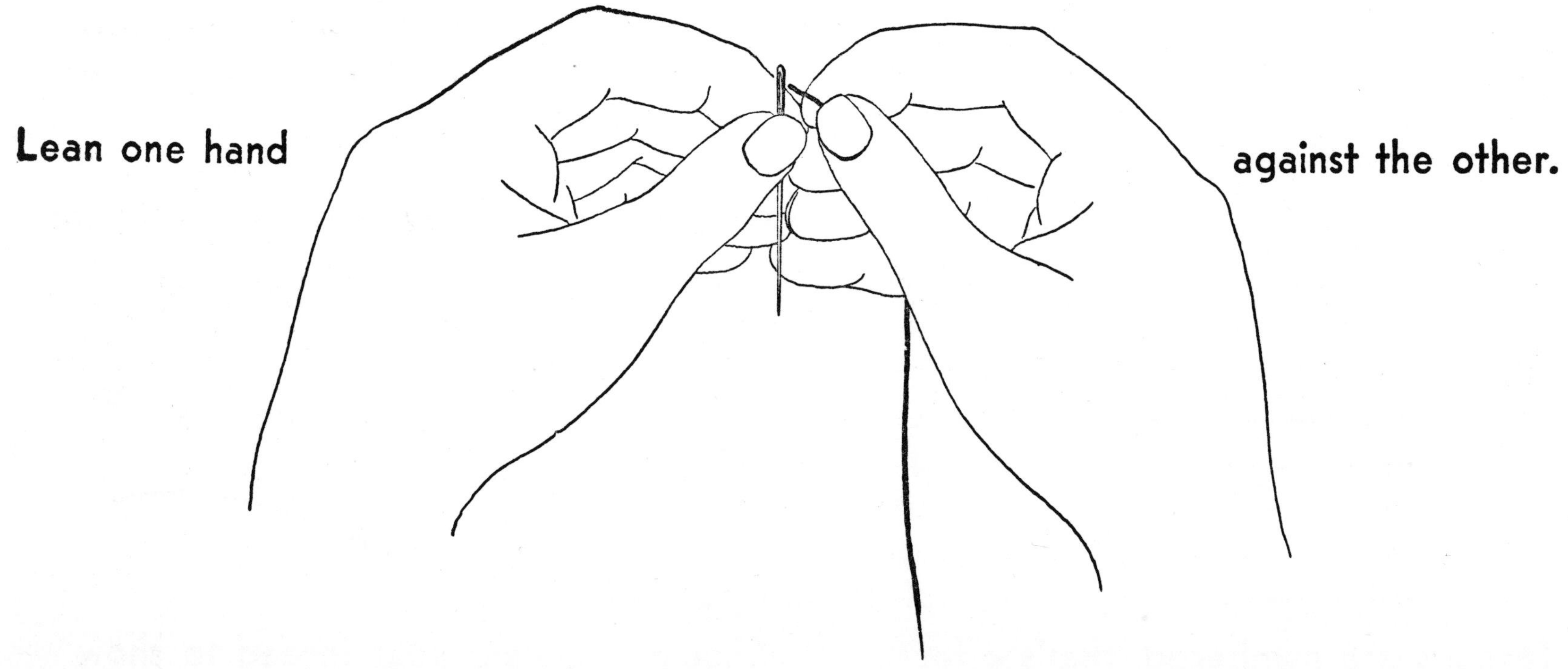

against the other.

Use thread the length of your arm. Thread the end nearest the spool.
If you can't see the needle's eye, hold it against the light or something white.

# HOW TO MAKE A KNOT

Wind thread around tip of forefinger of left hand, like this . . .

Twirl twice with thumb. Push thumb forward.

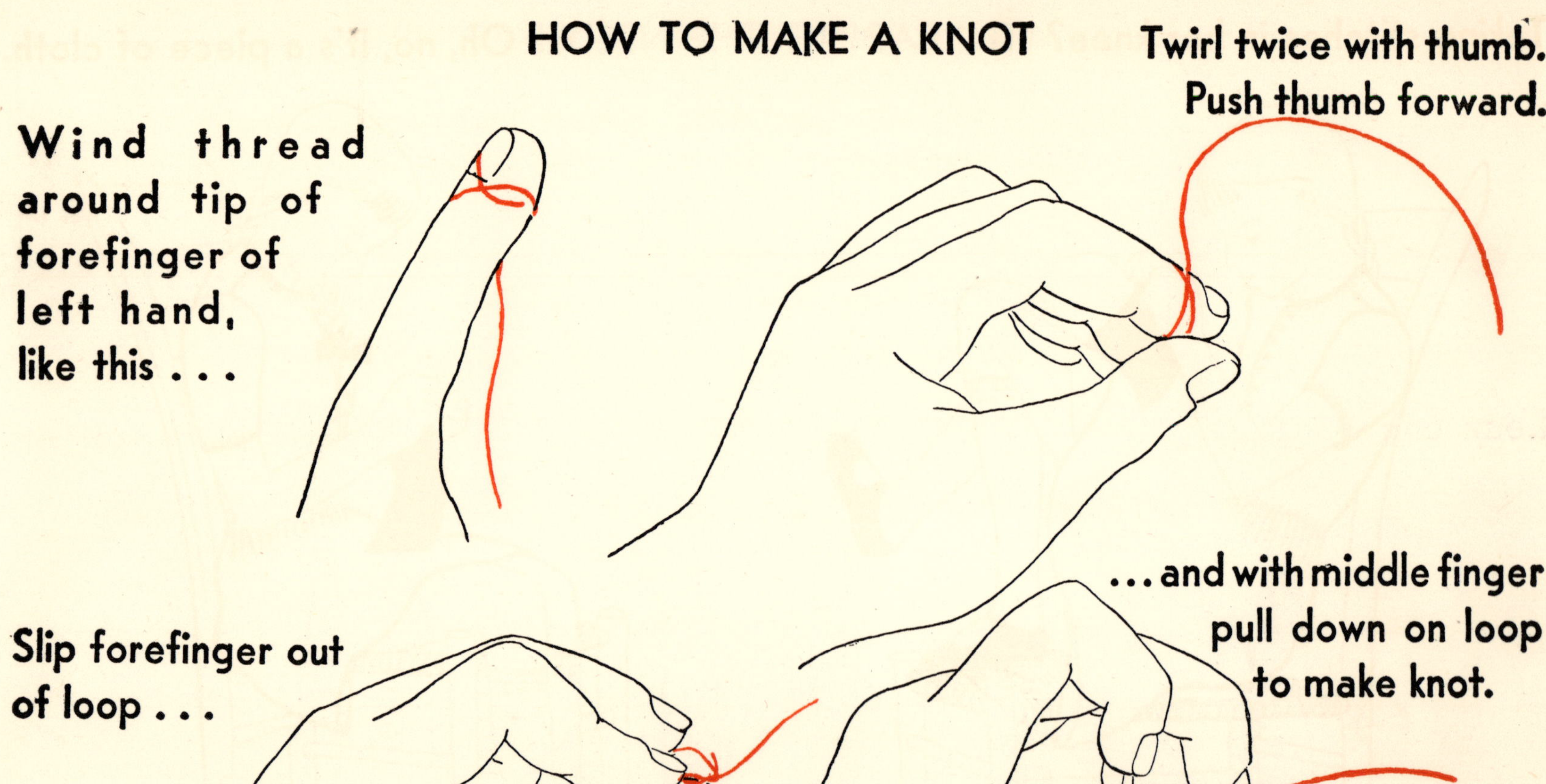

Slip forefinger out of loop . . .

. . . and with middle finger pull down on loop to make knot.

A perfect knot is the size of a pinhead . . . without frills.

Taking stitches in her knee?

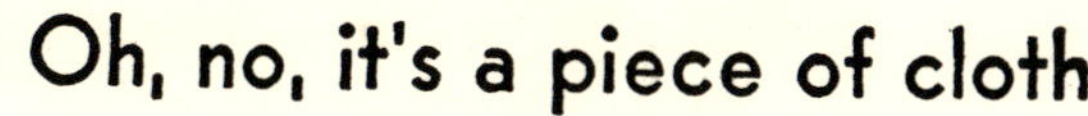

Oh, no, it's a piece of cloth.

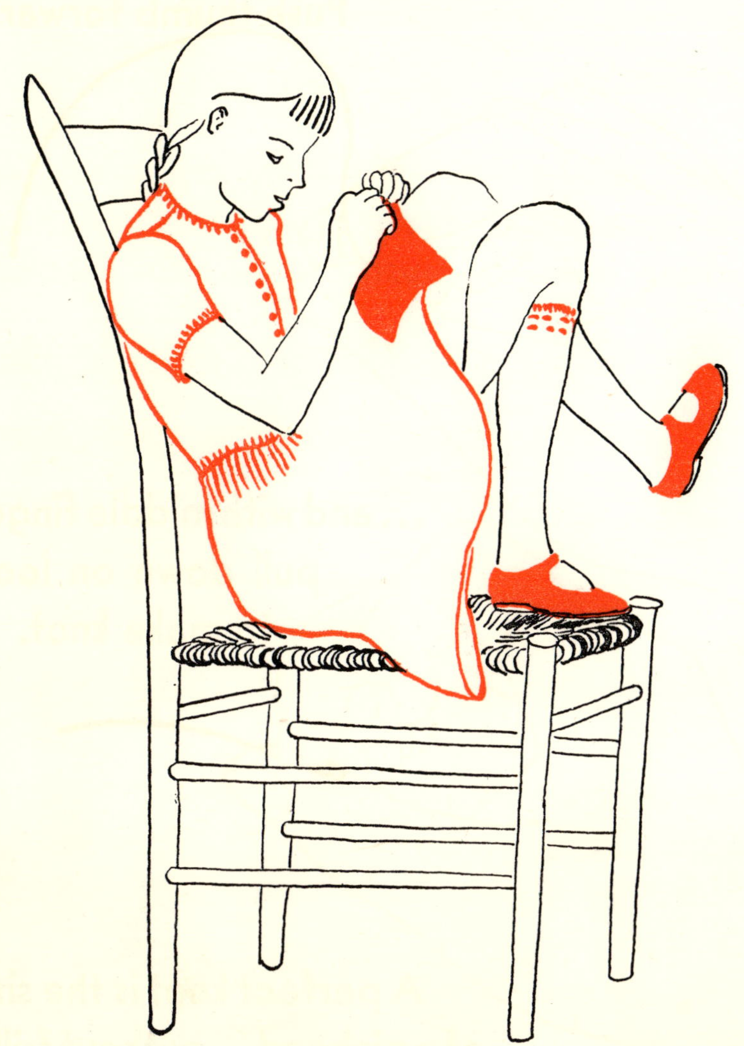

# THIMBLES NEED NOT BE A NUISANCE

Only tailors can use a thimble without a top.
They push the needle in with the side of the thimble.

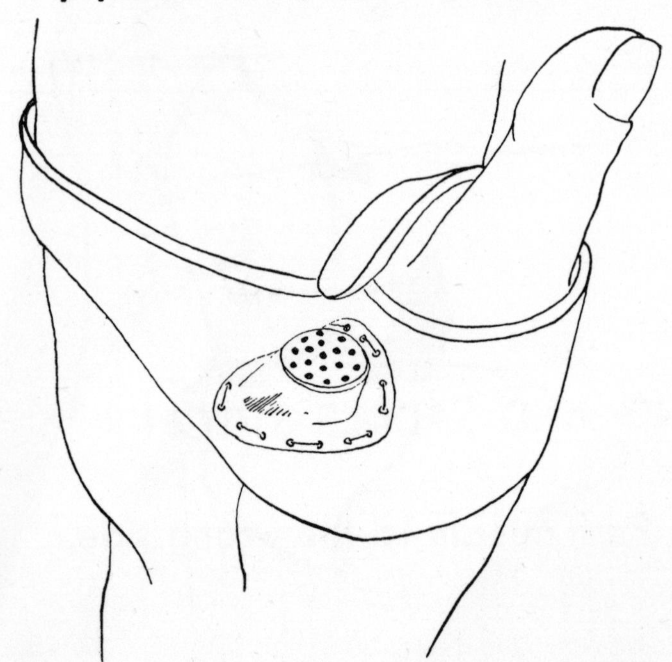

A sailor straps his on his thumb. They use enormous needles for making sails and need the whole hand to push the needle through.

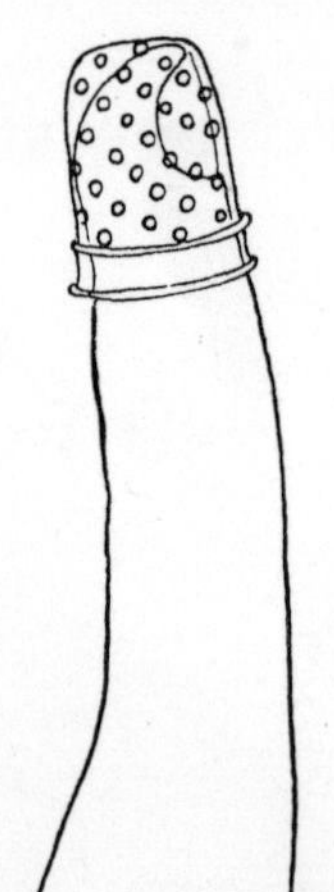

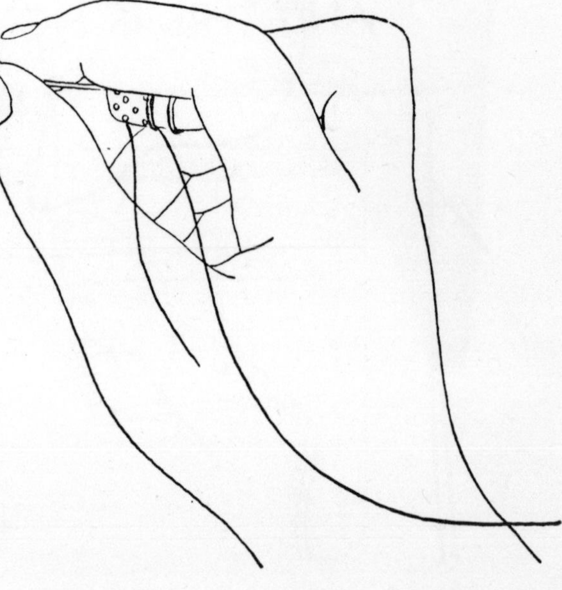

We use one that fits our middle finger so top of thimble touches tip of finger. Hold your needle in the middle. Push with thimble. If you have trouble, try a shorter needle, and push with side of thimble. Pull the needle out with thumb and forefinger. It takes longer to wear a hole in a thimble than in your fingertip.

# HOW TO START SEWING WITHOUT A KNOT

Take a stitch on the needle 1/4 inch from the edge. Pull thread through to within 1/2 inch of the end. This we cut off later.

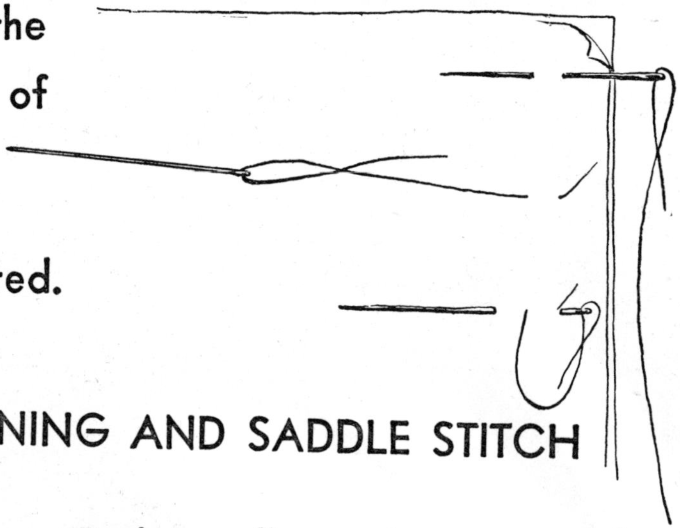

Take a stitch back to where the first one started. Then start sewing.

## AND THIS IS HOW TO END RUNNING AND SADDLE STITCH

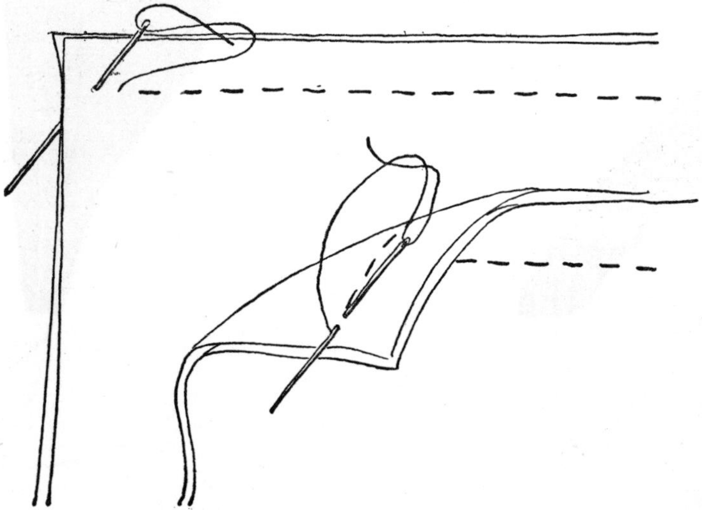

Push needle to the wrong side.

Under the last stitch, take up a few threads of the material. Take a few stitches in the same place. Cut thread.

# CREASING A FOLD

Creasing is done flat on the table (a cleared table, of course). It is the pressing down of folded material with the thumbs. A crease can serve as a guide-line for sewing or cutting. A crease will also flatten seams before pressing.

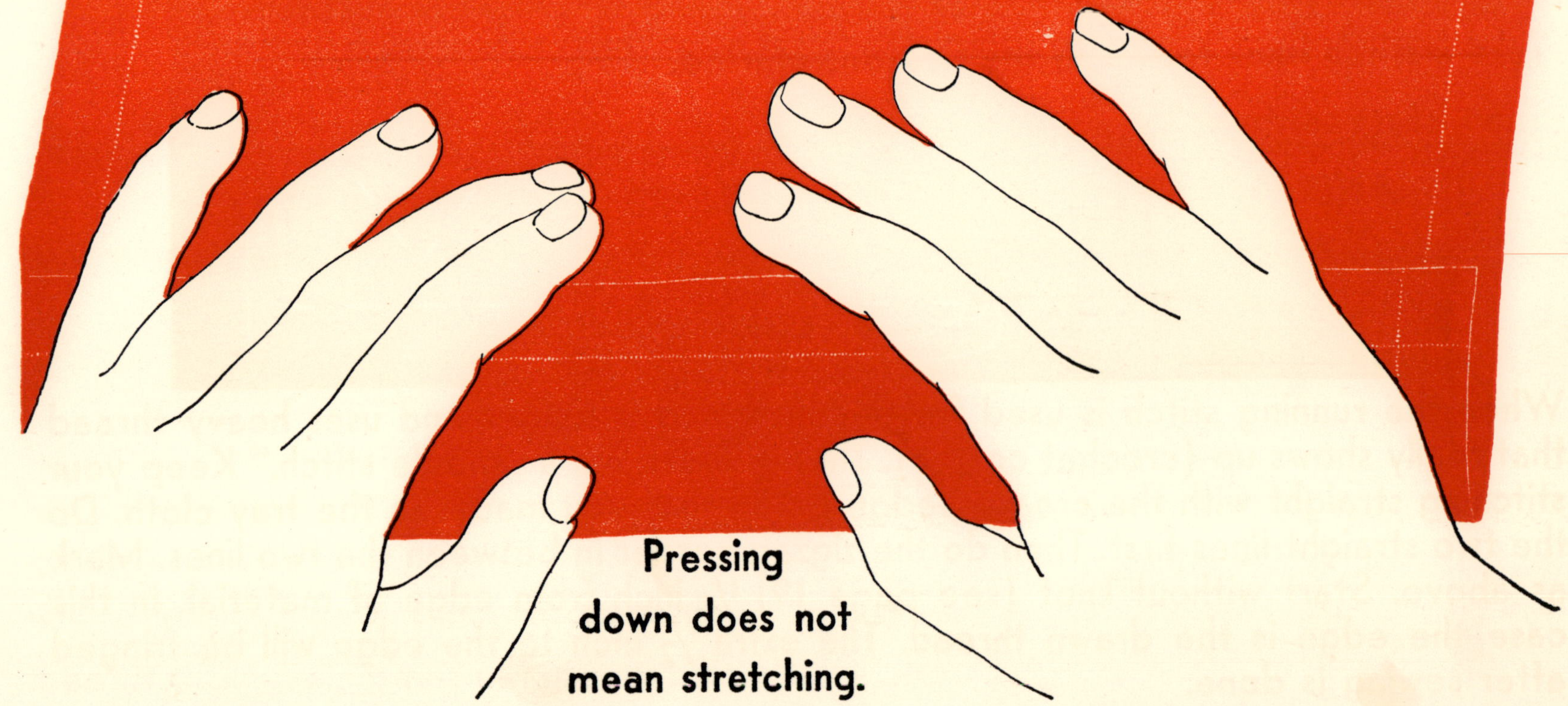

Pressing down does not mean stretching.

# DRESSING UP THE TRAY CLOTH

When the running stitch is used for decoration, it is longer and uses heavy thread that really shows up (crochet cotton). Then it looks like a "saddle stitch." Keep your stitching straight with the creased-edge guide that you made on the tray cloth. Do the two straight lines first. Then do the zigzag border in between the two lines. Mark as above. Start without knot (see page 19) 1/4 inch from edge of material. In this case the edge is the drawn thread. The extra 1/2 inch to the edge will be fringed after sewing is done.

# WHEN DOES A RUNNING STITCH RUN?

It is up to you. It's a quick and easy stitch. But you have to make it run yourself.

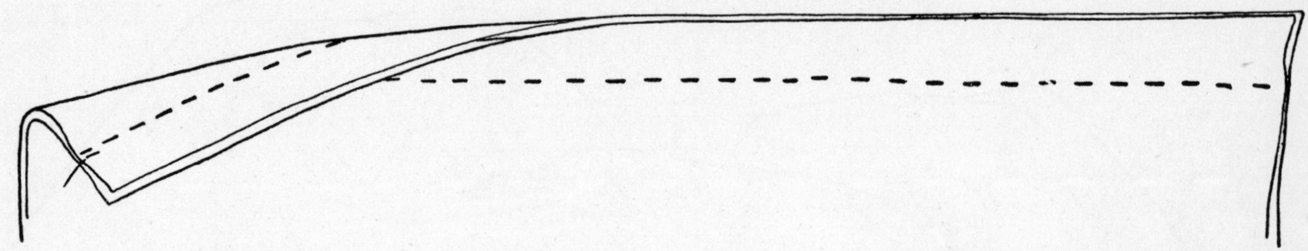

The length of the stitches and the length between them should be the same, 1/8 inch. A good running stitch looks the same on both sides. Start with a knot.

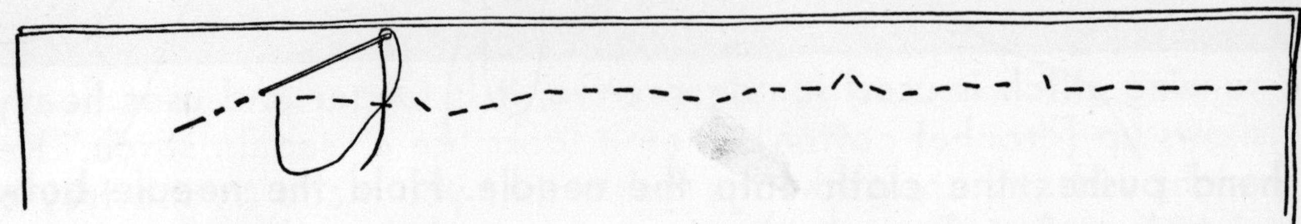

If your stitches are side-stepping, they are not running any more. If they go up and down hills, it means you have not followed your guide-line, the edge, or the thread of your material.

# HOW TO HOLD YOUR WORK FOR RUNNING STITCH

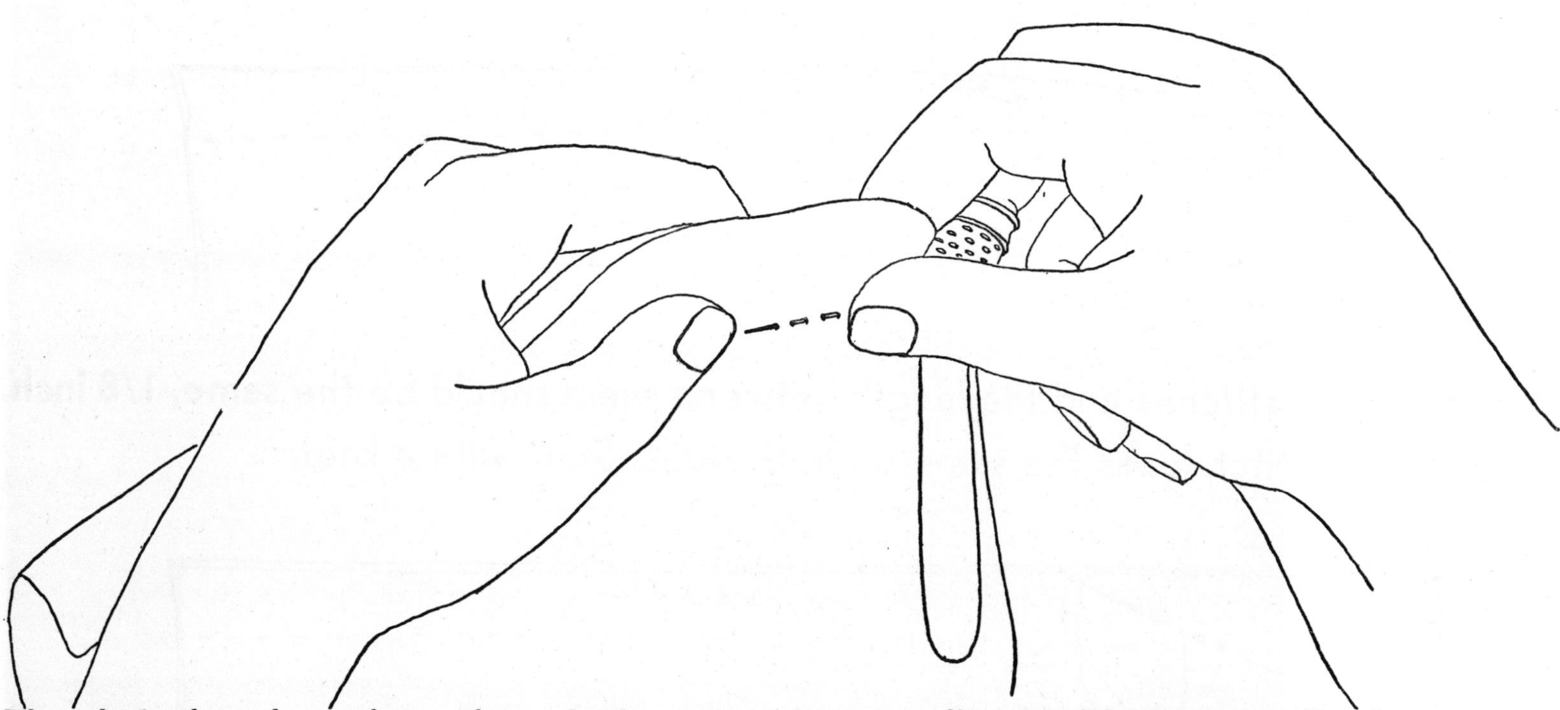

The left hand pushes the cloth onto the needle. Hold the needle between the forefinger and thumb, with the thumb on the right side. Take two stitches at a time. Later on when you can keep your stitches and spaces even, more stitches can be put on the needle. By the way, your thimble is your best friend in making running stitches.

Border designs are easy to make. A double line shows up well.

Just write your name in chalk. Start stitches from the right.

The Greeks called this "meander."

Your own design. Lines should not cross each other.

If you have any pet ideas of your own and want to make something else in the stitch you just learned, why don't you make a bureau scarf? Place your design in the center. Just fold your cloth the long way, then the short way, and crease. Draw your favorite animal in the center and stitch around it.

A luncheon set of six mats would be quickly made by doing a row of stitching around and putting a star in each corner, one point of the star facing the corner. Cut a cardboard star to trace from. Chalking it around will do the trick.

If you've decided by now that you like stitching (or fringing, as you will), there are lots of things that you can make, and no end to the ideas you'll get. For instance, you can make a set of napkins with the initials of the person who will receive them. Or perhaps a fruit outlined in one corner.

# WHY DO YOU GET SNAGS?

These little things are called snags. You get them most often when you are in a hurry because: 1. Your thread may be too long.
2. You may have threaded your needle with the wrong end of the thread. Thread is wound on the spool in such a way that it unwinds in the sewing when it is threaded on the wrong end. Always thread the end just wound off the spool.

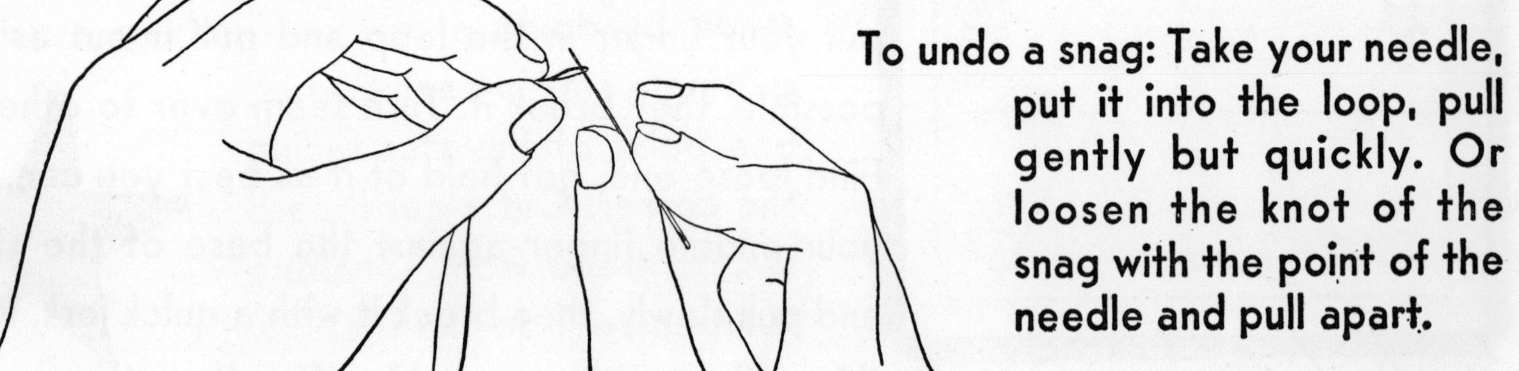

To undo a snag: Take your needle, put it into the loop, pull gently but quickly. Or loosen the knot of the snag with the point of the needle and pull apart.

## RIPPING MACHINE STITCHING BY HAND

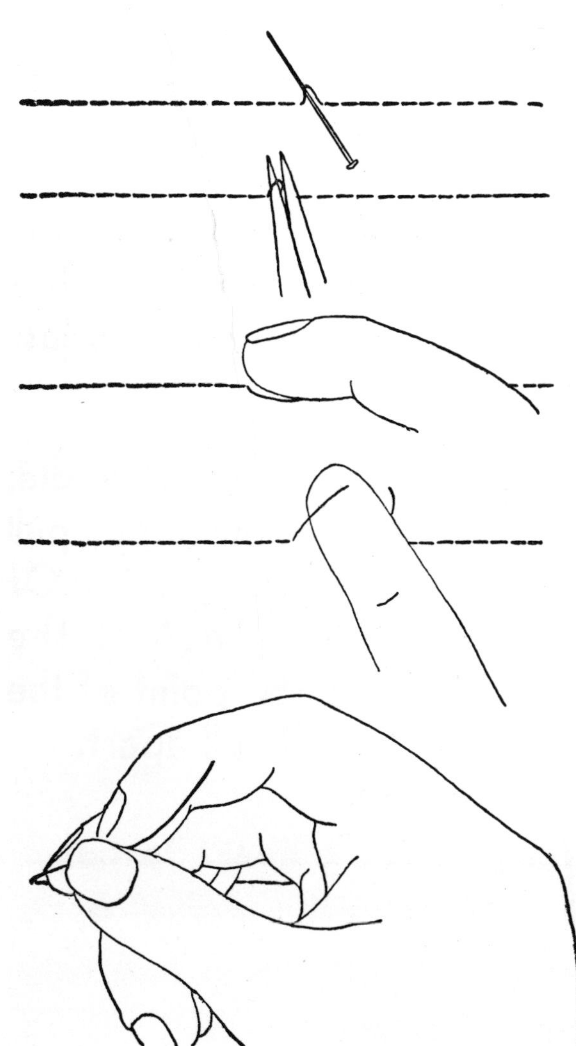

Place pin point under one stitch and pull it up gently but firmly. Don't break the thread if you can help it. When you have pulled up a loop big enough to hold your finger or the end of your scissors, cut or break thread. Then turn seam over.

Scratch up the loosened thread with your fingernail, put your finger in the loop and pull it out as far as possible, then break it. Turn seam over to other side. Find loose end, get hold of it as best you can, brace your middle finger against the base of the stitches and pull slowly, then break it with a quick jerk. Repeat this on both sides, one side after the other, until the seam is ripped out. You will find that the thread is always longer on the other side from the one you have just worked on, but that's the fun of the game.

# A PINCUSHION IN AN HOUR

You can make this pincushion in an hour. A few more minutes will make it even neater.

Materials needed:

¼ yard of quaint print; percale, old-fashioned calico or challis. About two cups of sawdust. Two arms' lengths of yarn.

(In a color matching one in the print, or just a gay color.)

If you have an outgrown dress that you don't mind cutting up, that's fine. The sleeves will be enough. The rest of the dress you can use for something else. It takes a heart to cut a heart out of something you once wore and loved. But this is one way of remembering.

# CUT YOUR HEART OUT

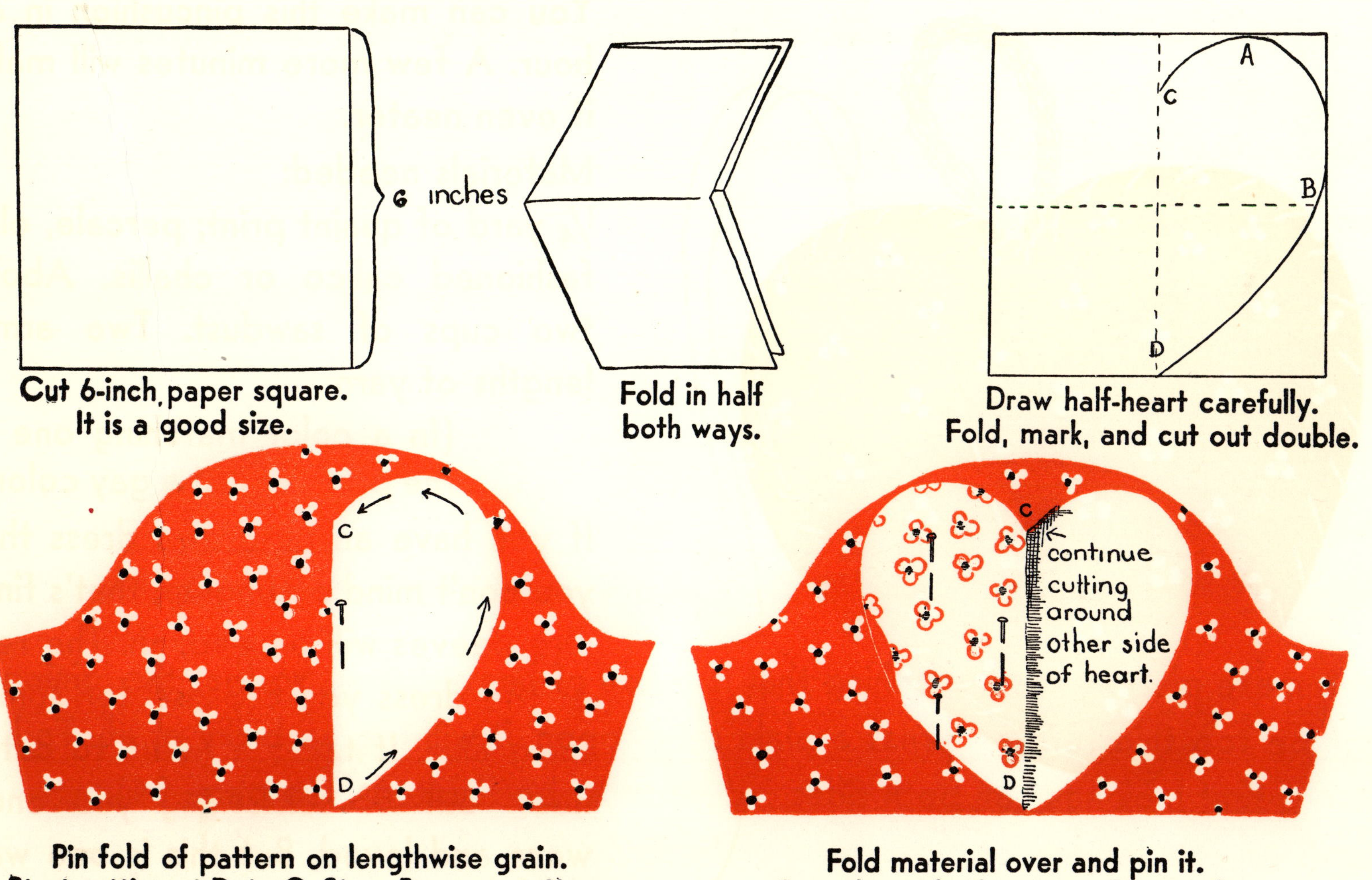


Cut 6-inch paper square.
It is a good size.

Fold in half
both ways.

Draw half-heart carefully.
Fold, mark, and cut out double.

Pin fold of pattern on lengthwise grain.
Start cutting at D, to C. Stop. Remove pattern.

Fold material over and pin it.
Cut other side the same. Cut 2 sides.

# TO SEW A FINE SEAM

A seam joins together two pieces of material. It is usually basted together first, then sewn with whatever stitch will hold it best.
The simplest of seams is the plain seam.

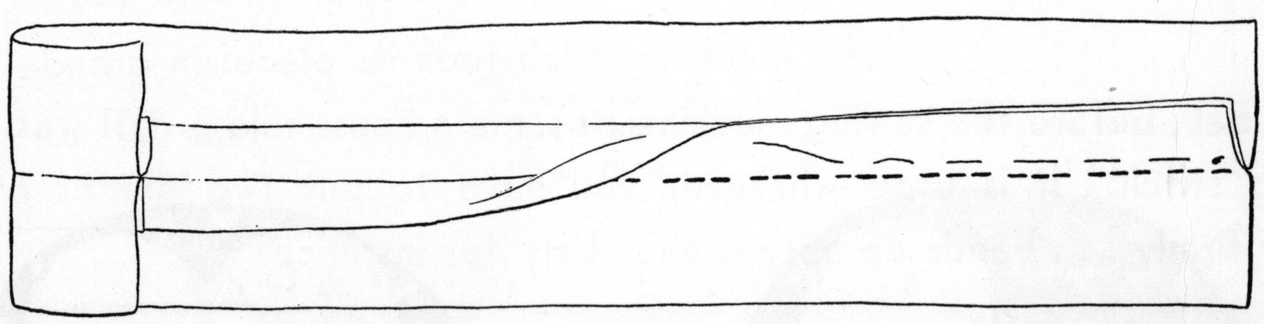

We make plain seams in clothing that is made of heavy fabric, so that the joining will not be too thick. If you press a plain seam open, it will not be bulky at all. To have seams that look neat on both sides, edges must be finished (see page 34).
Look at the insides of your own clothing to see how many kinds of seams and finishings you can discover.

# BACKSTITCHING

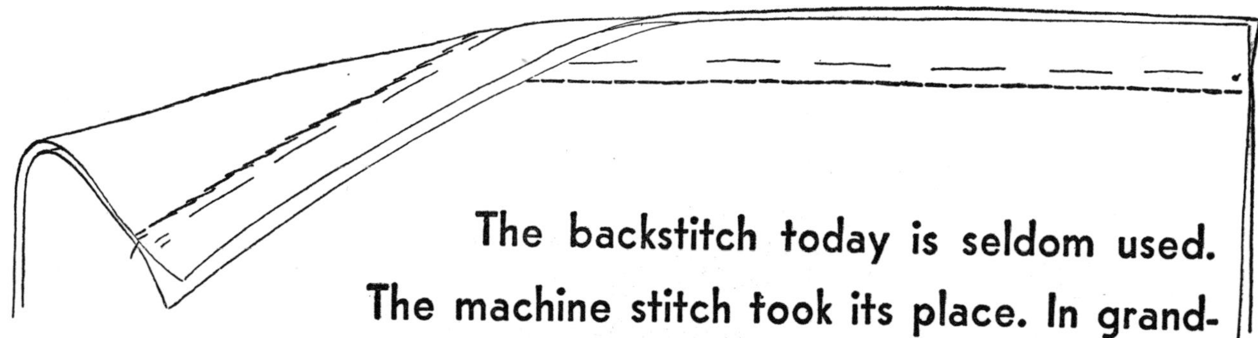

The backstitch today is seldom used. The machine stitch took its place. In grandmother's day, before the sewing machine became a household pet, it was called the "stitching stitch." It is used wherever you have to put two pieces of material together firmly .... bands on aprons and skirts, for instance.

To begin: Slip your knot between two layers of cloth. Take a short stitch back and bring the needle one stitch forward. Now you make another backstitch meeting the last stitch. Repeat.

Do your stitches look machine-made? The back should look like a cord.

# HAND POSITIONS FOR BACKSTITCH AND COMBINATION STITCH

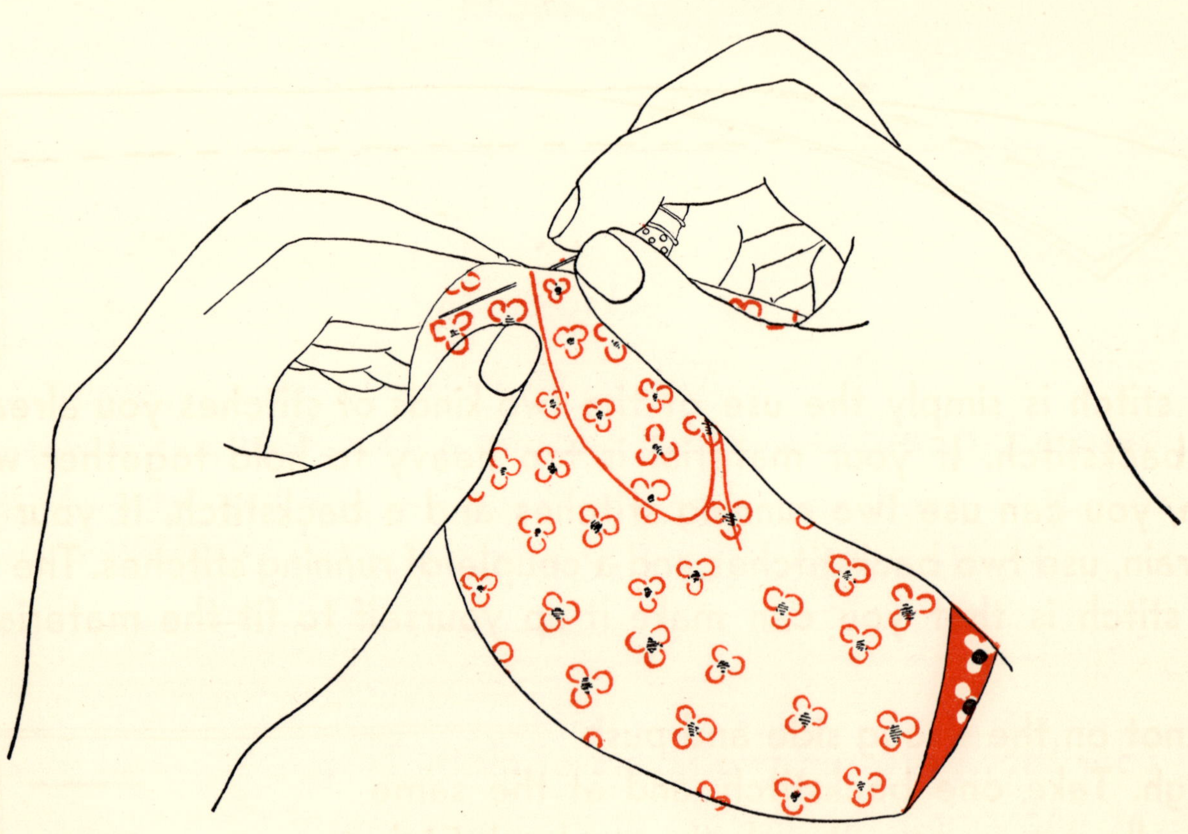

**Use the middle finger to hold down the material.**

# COMBINATION STITCH

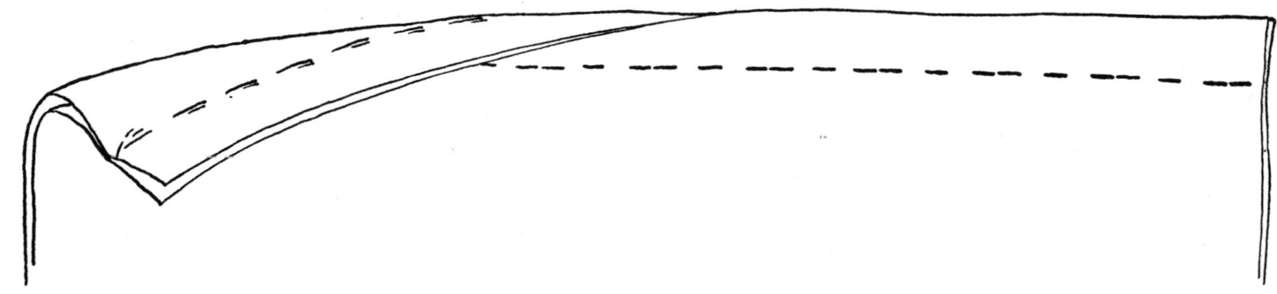

Combination stitch is simply the use of the two kinds of stitches you already know, running and backstitch. If your material is too heavy to hold together with just a running stitch, you can use two running stitches and a backstitch. If your seam will have extra strain, use two backstitches and a couple of running stitches. The fun about combination stitch is that you can make it up yourself to fit the material you are working on.

Start with a knot on the wrong side and push needle through. Take one backstitch, and at the same time push needle one space ahead of your backstitch. Now take another backstitch, come out a space ahead again and take two running stitches on your needle. Now repeat. One backstitch, two running stitches, etc.

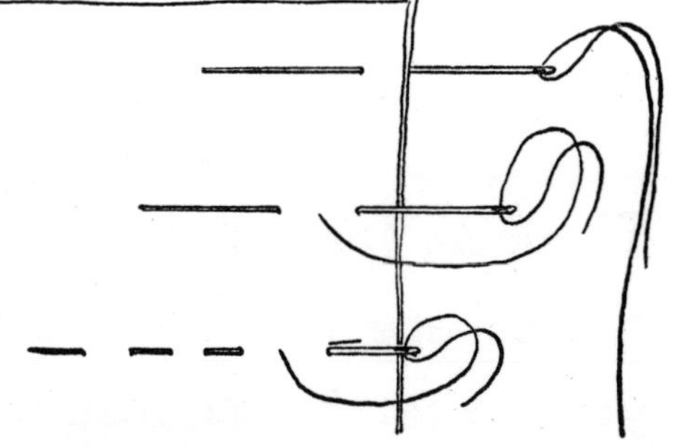

# OVERCASTING

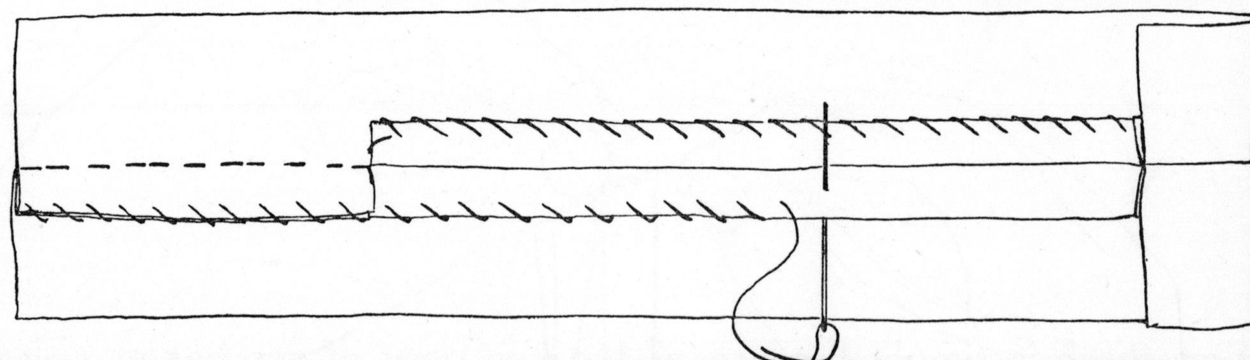

Overcasting is a large stitch. It is used to stop edges from raveling. Two edges of a seam may be overcast together, or pressed open and overcast singly. Hold it as you do overhanding (see opposite page). Start with a knot. Go from right to left. You can also go from left to right. Keep stitches 1/4 inch apart and 1/4 inch deep. At the corners take two stitches in the same place.

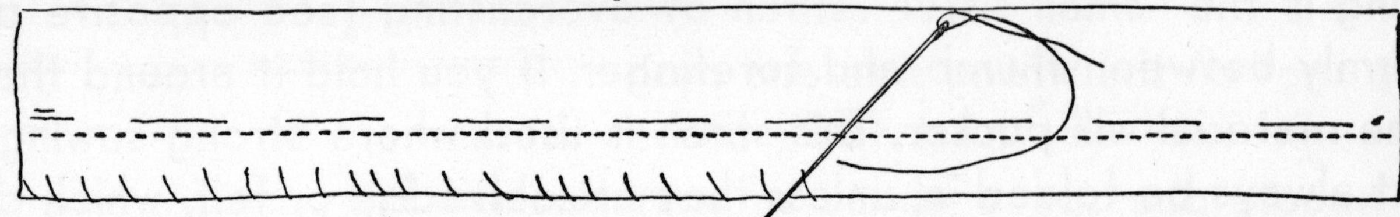

To finish thread, take two tiny stitches in the seam. Start where the last stitch ended. If you are ten years old and your overcasting looks like this, you're doing well for your age. Remember to keep stitches and spaces between them equal in length.

# OVERHANDING AND HOW TO HOLD IT

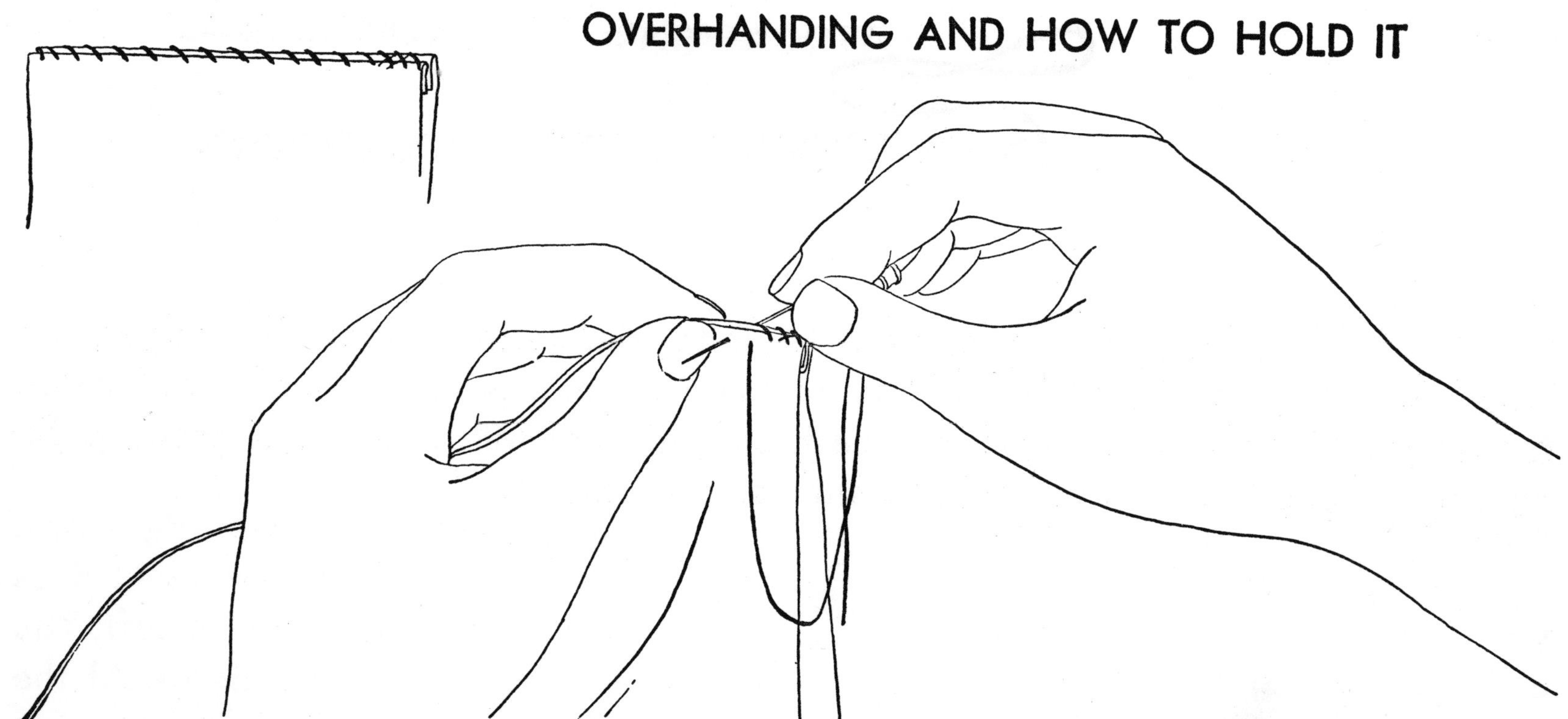

Overhanding is the "small sister" stitch of overcasting (see opposite page). Hold material firmly between thumb and forefinger. If you hold it around the finger one layer of the material will pucker. This stitch is used where strong sewing is needed. Edges must always be folded in, unless they are selvedge or felt, which do not ravel. Begin without a knot. Leave about ½ inch of thread. With the help of your needle, lay this on top of the folded edges. Sew over it with two tiny stitches. End the same way.

## SHOWING OFF OVERCASTING

Overcasting can be pretty to look at. Use it to trim sewed edges. Felt edges, for instance, will not ravel. Use embroidery cotton or yarn. Unwind piece of yarn 3 times the length of the edge you will overcast, so that yarn will last without piecing. To end, slip thread between the finished stitches underneath.

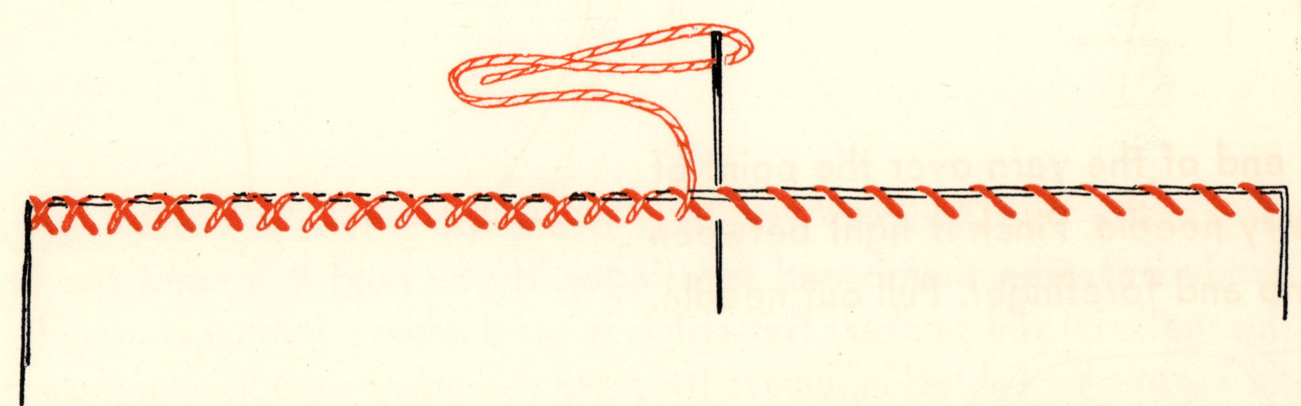

Double overcasting makes a fancier finish. You simply go back the way you came, taking stitches between each overcasting. This will form a line of crosses on each side of the seam. Using two colors makes this especially pretty. Finish the ends well.

# THREADING YARN OR TAPESTRY NEEDLE

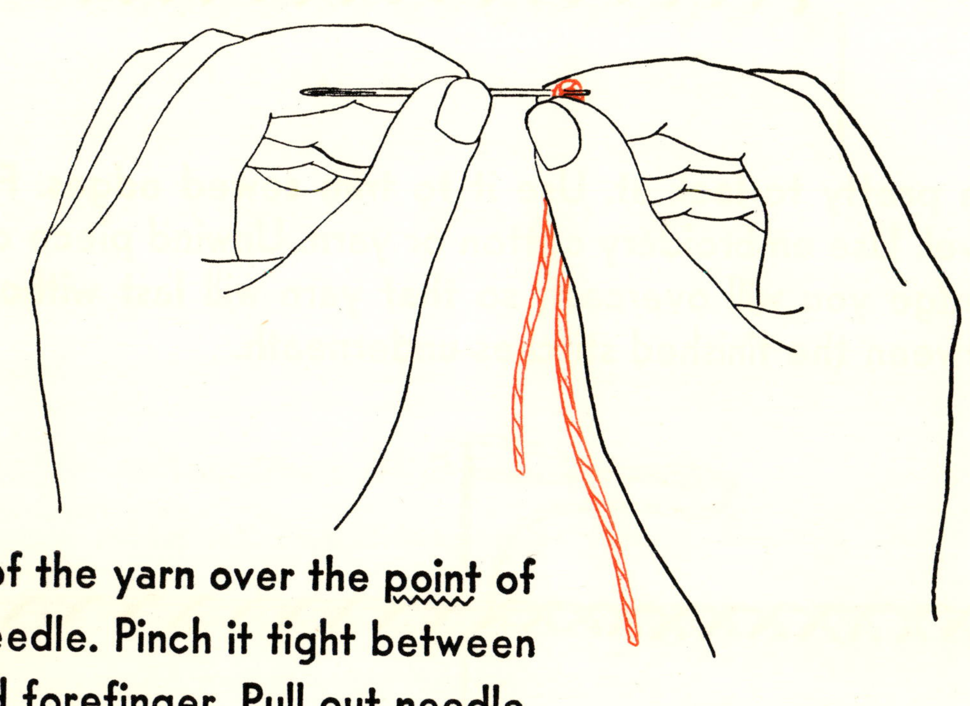

Loop the end of the yarn over the point of the tapestry needle. Pinch it tight between your thumb and forefinger. Pull out needle.

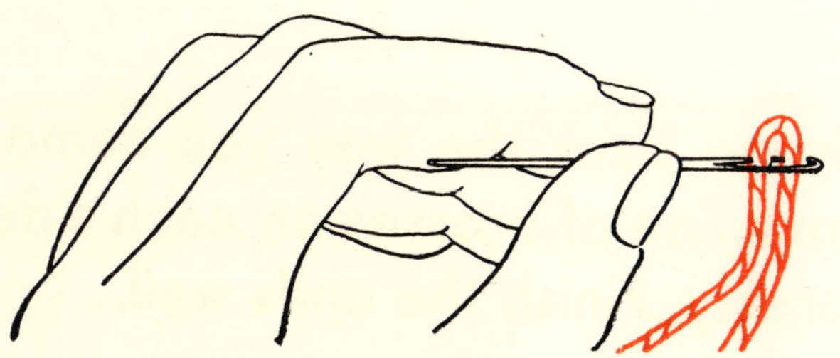

Turn needle around. Now this double flattened end can be pushed through the eye easily.

## NOW YOU CAN SEW YOUR PINCUSHION

Decide which is the pretty or right side of your printed material. Place right sides facing each other. Start with a knot. Put the needle 1/4 inch from the edge at letter A. Take one backstitch.

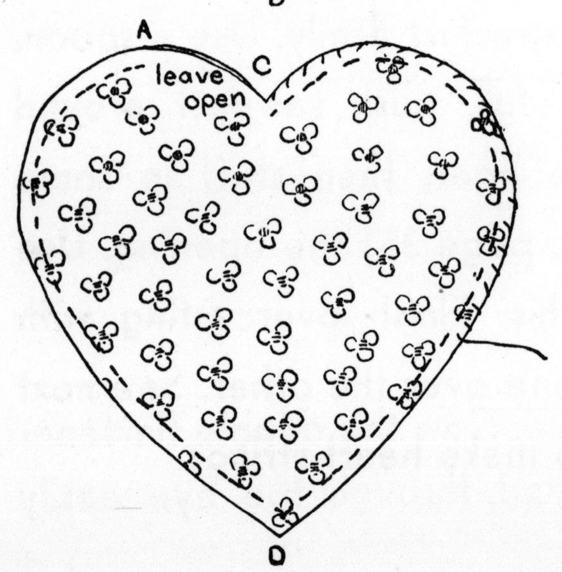


Sew around with combination stitch (see pages 32-33). Keep stitches an even 1/4 inch from the edge. When you reach C, finish thread by trying overcasting on your seam for practice (see page 35). Keep the overcasting outside of your combination-stitch seam. Remember that the outside overcasting will have to be done very neatly.

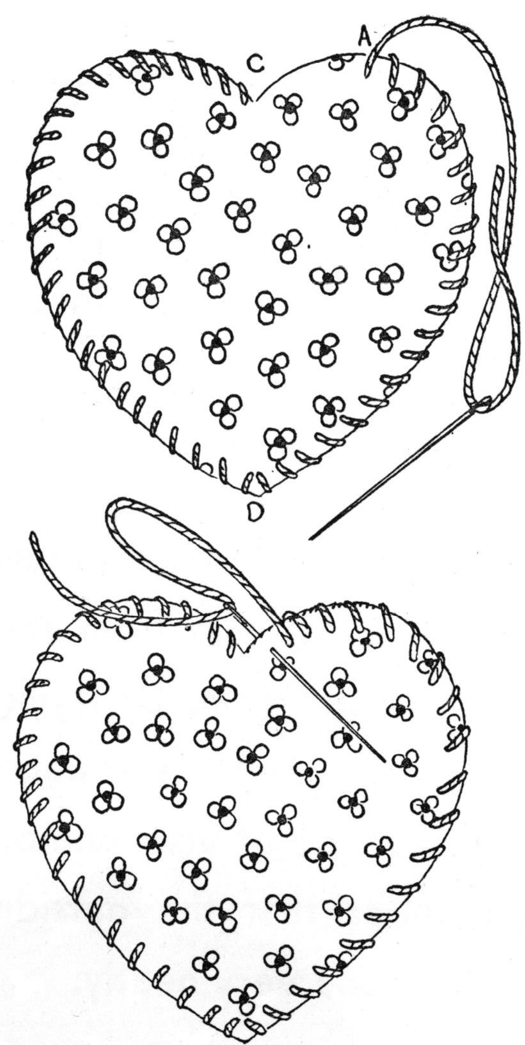


## ALMOST DONE NOW

Turn your "heart" inside out. Push the edges of the seam out with your fingers, specially at D. Thread your yarn-needle (see page 31) in the gaily-colored yarn you selected. Hide the knot at C inside the seam. Overcast around and stop at A.

Stuff pincushion with sawdust firmly. Use a spoon. When you think it's full, push sawdust around seam with your forefinger, then stuff in some more. Overhand (see page 35) the opening. Use double thread for this. Finish overcasting with three small stitches, one over the other. See next page to learn how to make heart-strings.

## HEART-STRINGS TO TUG

Take 3 small stitches to fasten a piece of yarn, as shown at left. Leave the fourth stitch loose enough so that you can make the next loop with the thumb and forefinger of the right hand. To tighten the loop, use left hand and tug on long end of the yarn.

You can use a crochet hook for this chain if you prefer.

When you have a heart-string 3 inches long, thread needle and fasten down with 3 small stitches where the string started.

## "A-RIDING WE WILL GO"

You can make this horse out of $1\frac{1}{2}$ yards of 36-inch wide chintz or flowered cretonne. He was born out of the head of a little girl of ten who made him by herself. His mane and tail are made of a ten-cent floor mop. The tail is braided, with a knot at the end, so it won't unravel. He is stuffed with shredded newspaper. His ears were dipped in jelly-jar wax. His big black eyes are appliquéd.

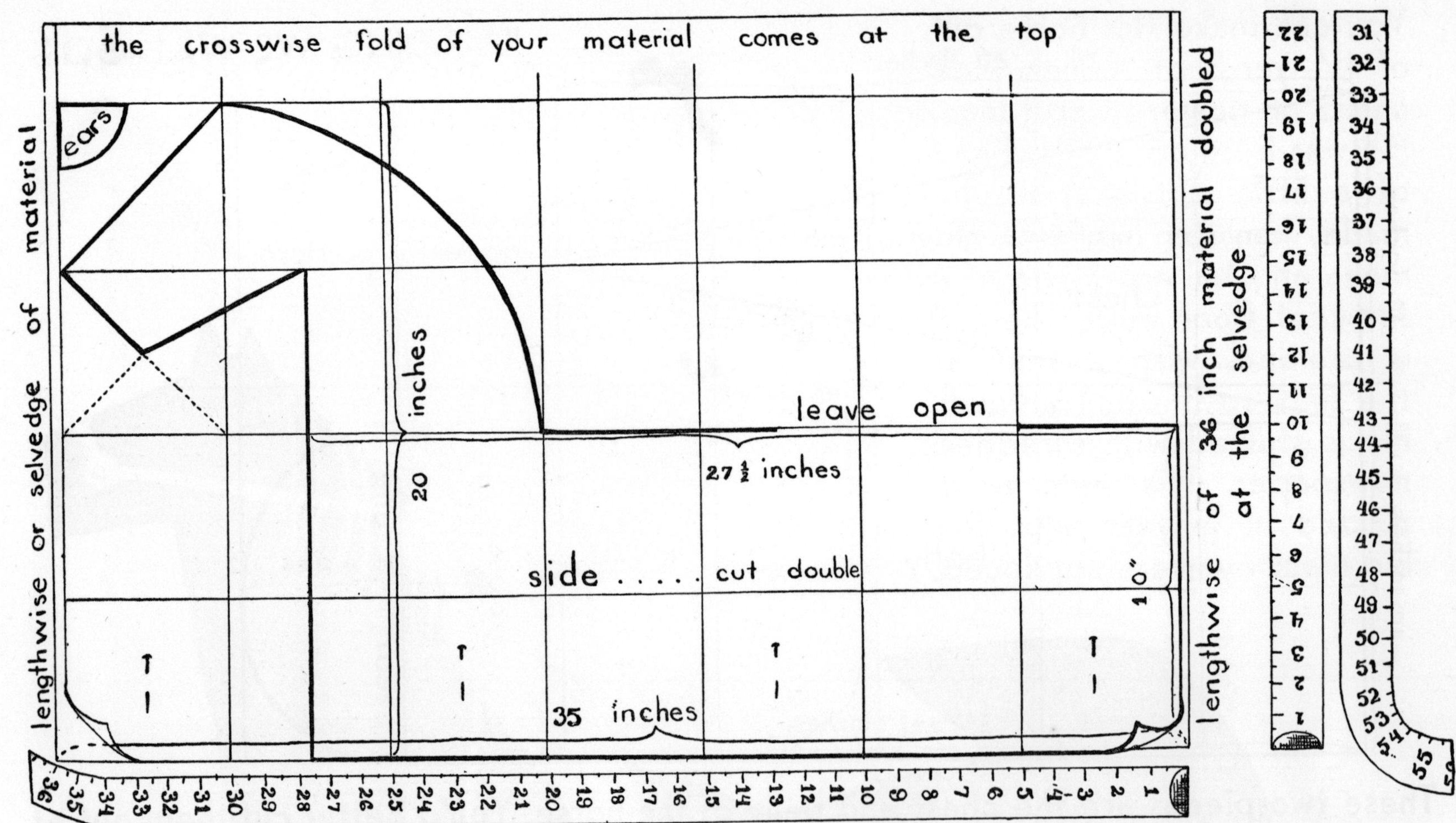


Make top and bottom edges of your 1½ yards of 36-inch material even. Draw your horse onto cloth divided into 5-inch squares for ease in measuring. Pin top and bottom edges of yardage together so you can cut both sides of the horse at once.

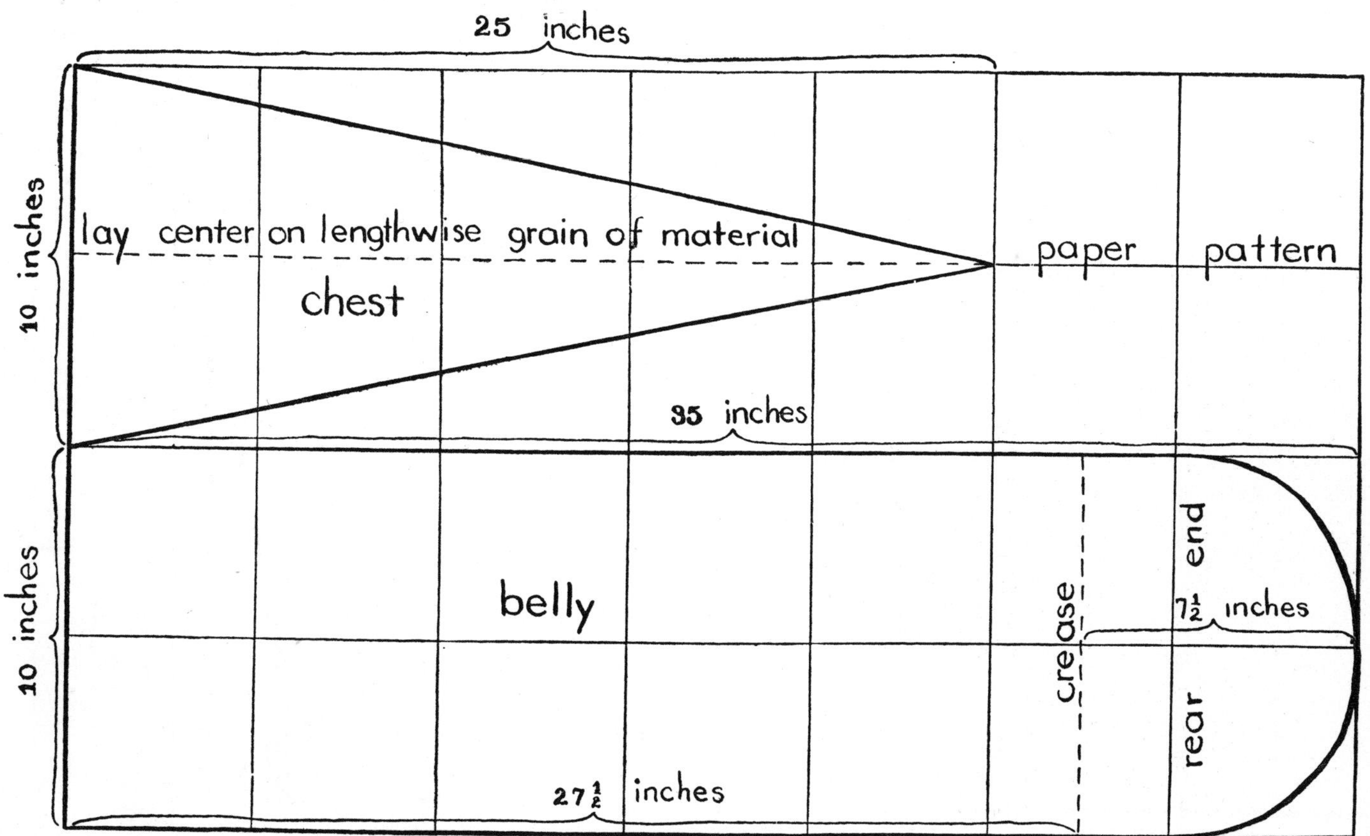


These two pieces are the chest and belly of the horse. You'd better cut them out of paper first. Just fold a sheet of paper 35 inches long and 20 inches wide into 5-inch squares. Draw the outlines on, and cut them out. Lay each on a single layer of cloth. You need only one of each. Watch the grain! Keep it straight with the edge of pattern.

## LET'S PUT THE HORSE TOGETHER

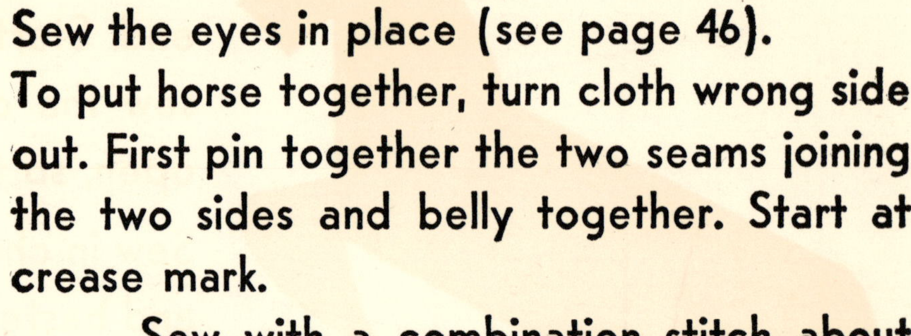

Sew the eyes in place (see page 46).
To put horse together, turn cloth wrong side out. First pin together the two seams joining the two sides and belly together. Start at crease mark.

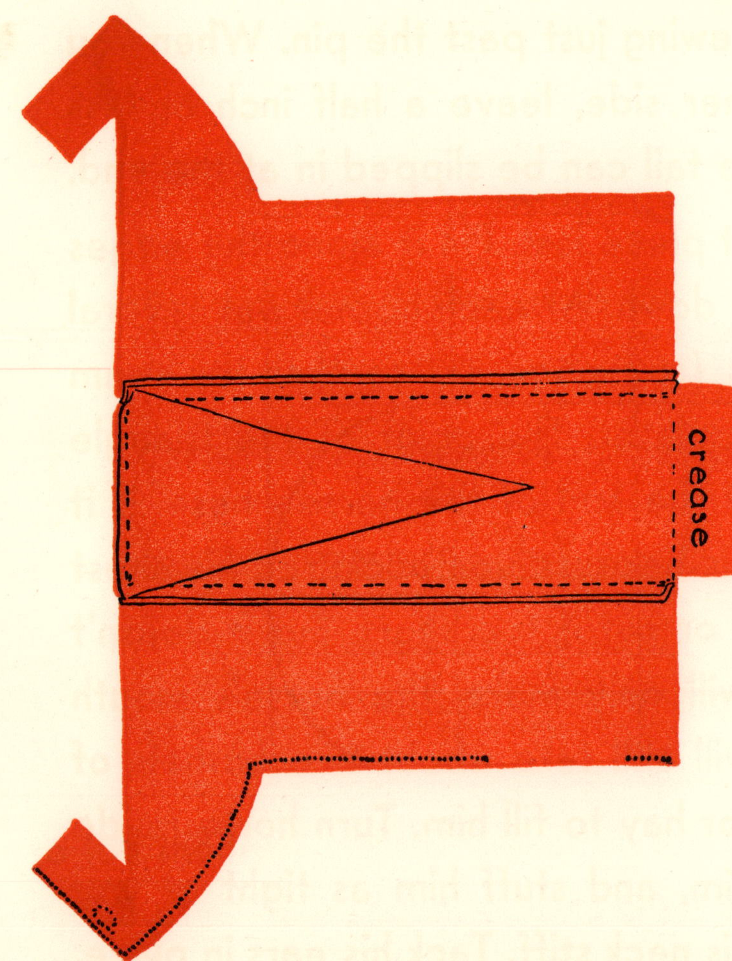


Sew with a combination stitch about 1/2 inch from the edge.

Sew belly and chest together.

Start all your seams with a backstitch, and end with two backstitches one atop the other, so that the sewing will hold.

Now sew up the spine (dotted line in drawing). Leave about a 6-inch opening so you can turn the horse right-side-out and stuff him. If you live in the country, you can stuff him with hay. Two bushels of stuffing will fill him nicely, and make him look well-fed.

Open up back seam and pin to center of rear end. Start sewing just past the pin. When you sew the other side, leave a half inch or less open, so the tail can be slipped in at the end.

Sew in chest piece last. Pin it along the edges and baste it down. At each corner put several backstitches (see page 31) so that the seam won't rip out later. The point of the triangle should meet the end of the horse's nose. If it does not, it is because you puckered his chest in sewing it, or cut it too short. But it doesn't matter. It will only make the horse's mouth smaller. It will still take about two bushels of newspaper or hay to fill him. Turn horse inside out. Stuff him, and stuff him as tight as you can. Make his neck stiff. Tack his ears in place. Overhand opening and remember the tail.

## THE TRICK OF APPLIQUE

The trick of appliqué is this: your material to be appliquéd must be cut on the same grain as the cloth you are sewing it onto. So . . . if the grain of the horse goes like this in this picture . . .

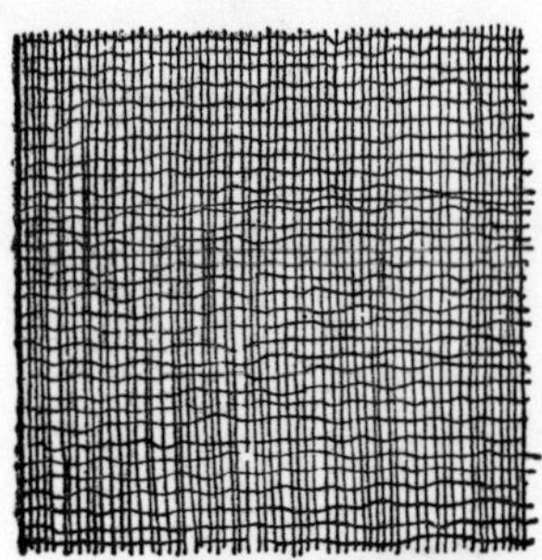

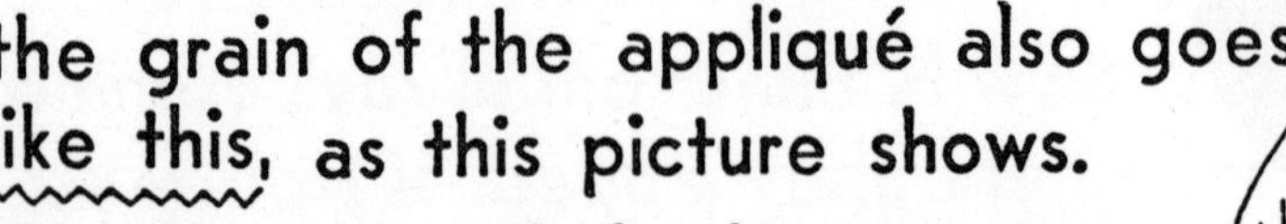

the grain of the appliqué also goes like this, as this picture shows.

For the eyes of the horse trace this shape and cut out of cardboard. Cut cloth (don't forget to match the grain) 1/8 inch larger than the cardboard. Then, holding cardboard on cloth, turn cloth edges under all around. Crease well. Pinch corners specially well. Be sure you cut two eyes. Remove cardboard and baste eyes to horse's head. Hold both sides of the head together to the light. Be sure both eyes are placed in the same position . . . unless, of course, you like cross-eyed horses.

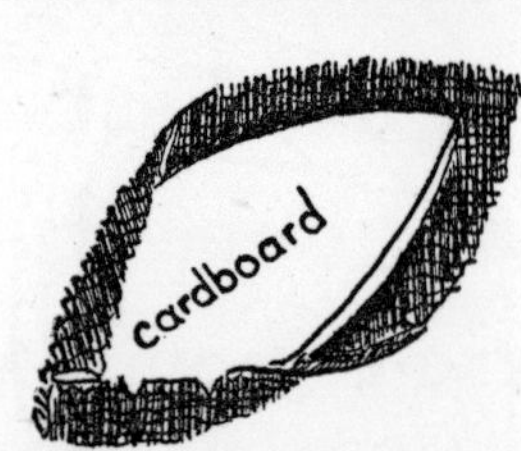


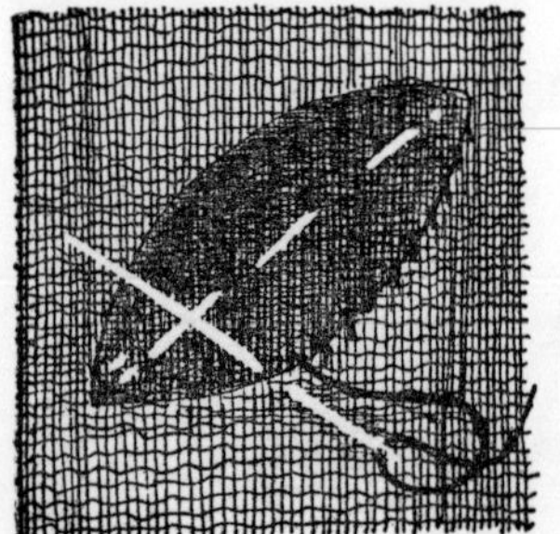

For most appliqué, you have to use matching thread. But not here. Make a knot, slip it under the folded edge. Take two tiny stitches at the corner to catch it down. Use small hemming stitches (58-59). Let your needle make the long slanting stitches underneath, but the slant should be short on top.

If crease unfolds, turn edges under with the point of the needle.

# OUTLINE STITCH

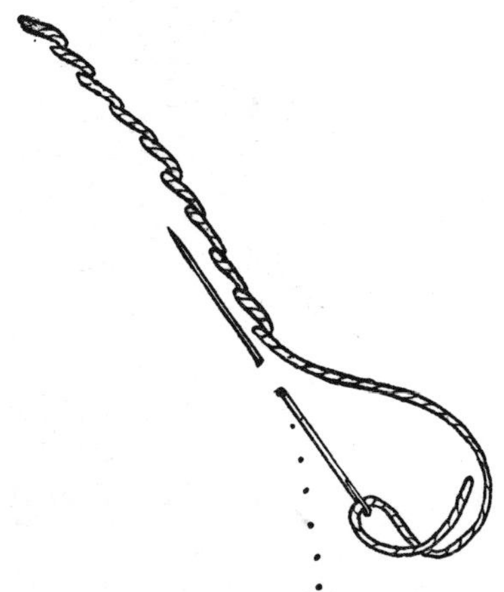

This is an embroidery stitch. Use embroidery yarn. Start with three running stitches, as shown. Cover them up with outline stitches. Keep thread to the right. Point needle to the left. Make your stitches even, always coming a little past where they ended. If you make your stitches too wide, you will be doing "stemstitching."

We can make use of outline stitch to sew on the horse's mane. Size of stitches can be 1/4 inch, with crochet cotton. Cut the strands of the mop, or rug yarn (whichever you decide to use), into equal pieces 8 inches long. Take your stitch. Before you pull your thread to finish it, slip one of the strands under it. If you stitch through the strand, it will never pull out.

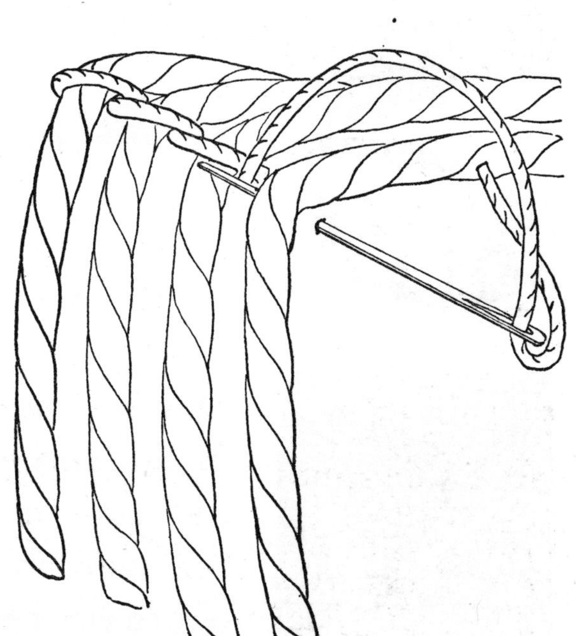

To complete the horse you only need about 2 yards of black twill tape for reins, which you can pull through two curtain rings tacked on the side of his mouth with an over-and-over stitch.

## IN CASE OF NEED

To make this first-aid kit easily washable, it is best to make it out of natural or khaki-color crash.

If you want to follow the cross-stitch pattern easily, use a basket-weave type of material. Half a yard will be enough to make three kits. (Other things to make the same way are suggested on page 62.)

For the cross-stitch pattern, buy a skein of cotton called "D. M. C. Embroidery Twist." It will look rich in body, and it behaves better than two or three strands of thinner cotton. It comes in lovely shades. The red is specially good. This yarn has a dull finish, which in fabric or thread is less gaudy, and so more beautiful. Let your work shine, not your material.

Notion counters in department stores carry the gay-colored twill tapes (about 1/2 inch wide) for tying up the kit.

# DESIGNING CROSS-STITCH

You can use your own drawing to make a cross-stitch pattern if you use checked paper. Let's say you have a cat, and like cats. Draw your pet on the checked paper in pencil.

Put a cross (in ink) into every square where the outline of your drawing fills the square more than halfway. If you are doing the drawing in two colors (the bow on the cat, for instance) use a crayon to make it show up.

Now erase your pencil drawing, leaving only the marked-in squares. Copy him on your material. Count the number of squares and make just that many stitches. You won't have trouble following your pattern if you use a coarse basket-weave type of material like monk's cloth, canvas, huck, or even burlap.

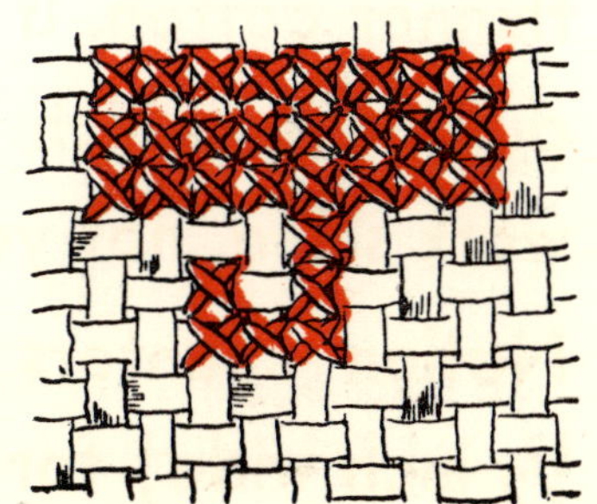

# CAN YOU PLAY . . .

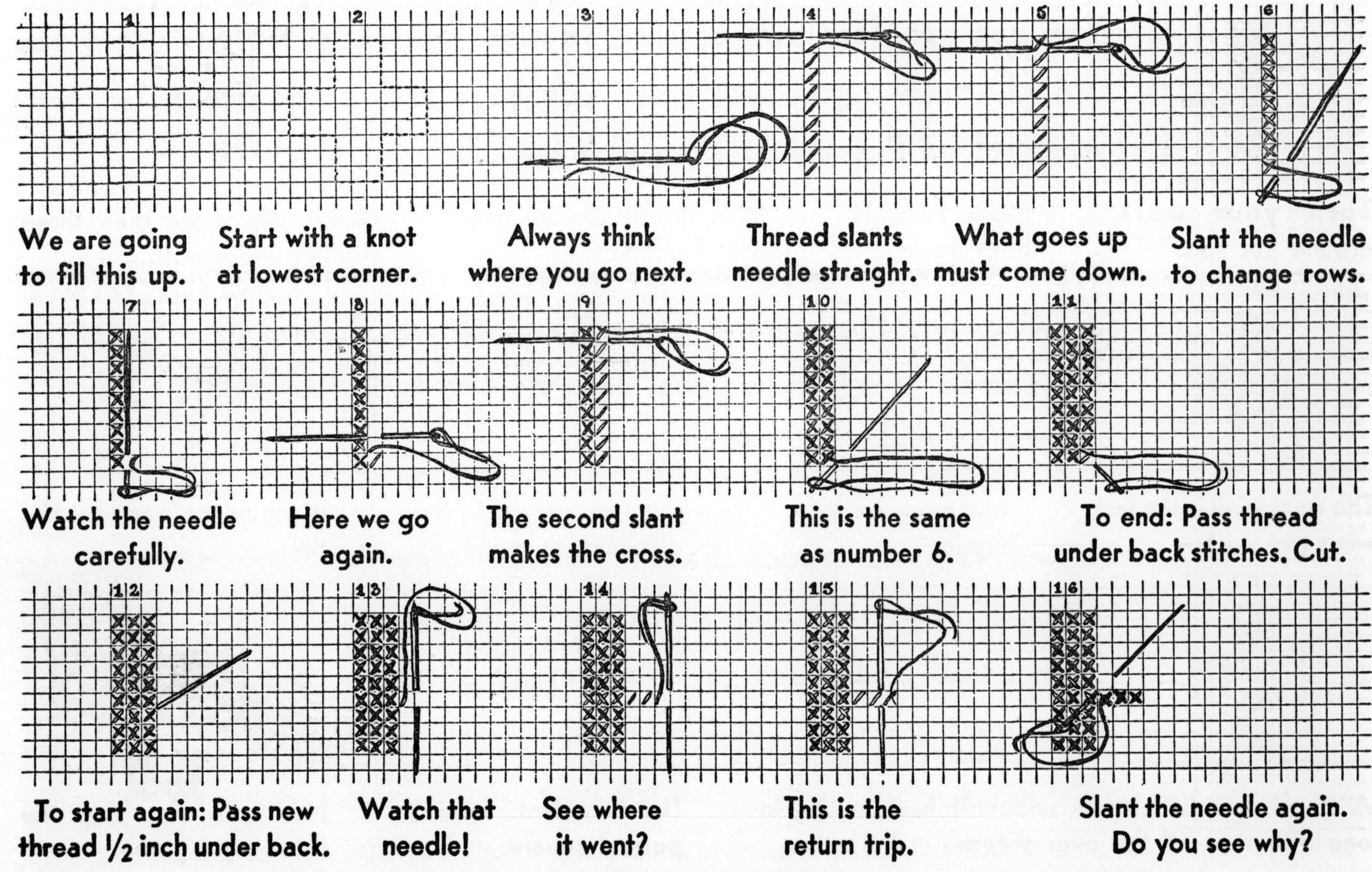

1. We are going to fill this up.
2. Start with a knot at lowest corner.
3. Always think where you go next.
4. Thread slants needle straight.
5. What goes up must come down.
6. Slant the needle to change rows.
7. Watch the needle carefully.
8. Here we go again.
9. The second slant makes the cross.
10. This is the same as number 6.
11. To end: Pass thread under back stitches. Cut.
12. To start again: Pass new thread 1/2 inch under back.
13. Watch that needle!
14. See where it went?
15. This is the return trip.
16. Slant the needle again. Do you see why?

## . . . THE CROSS-STITCH GAME?

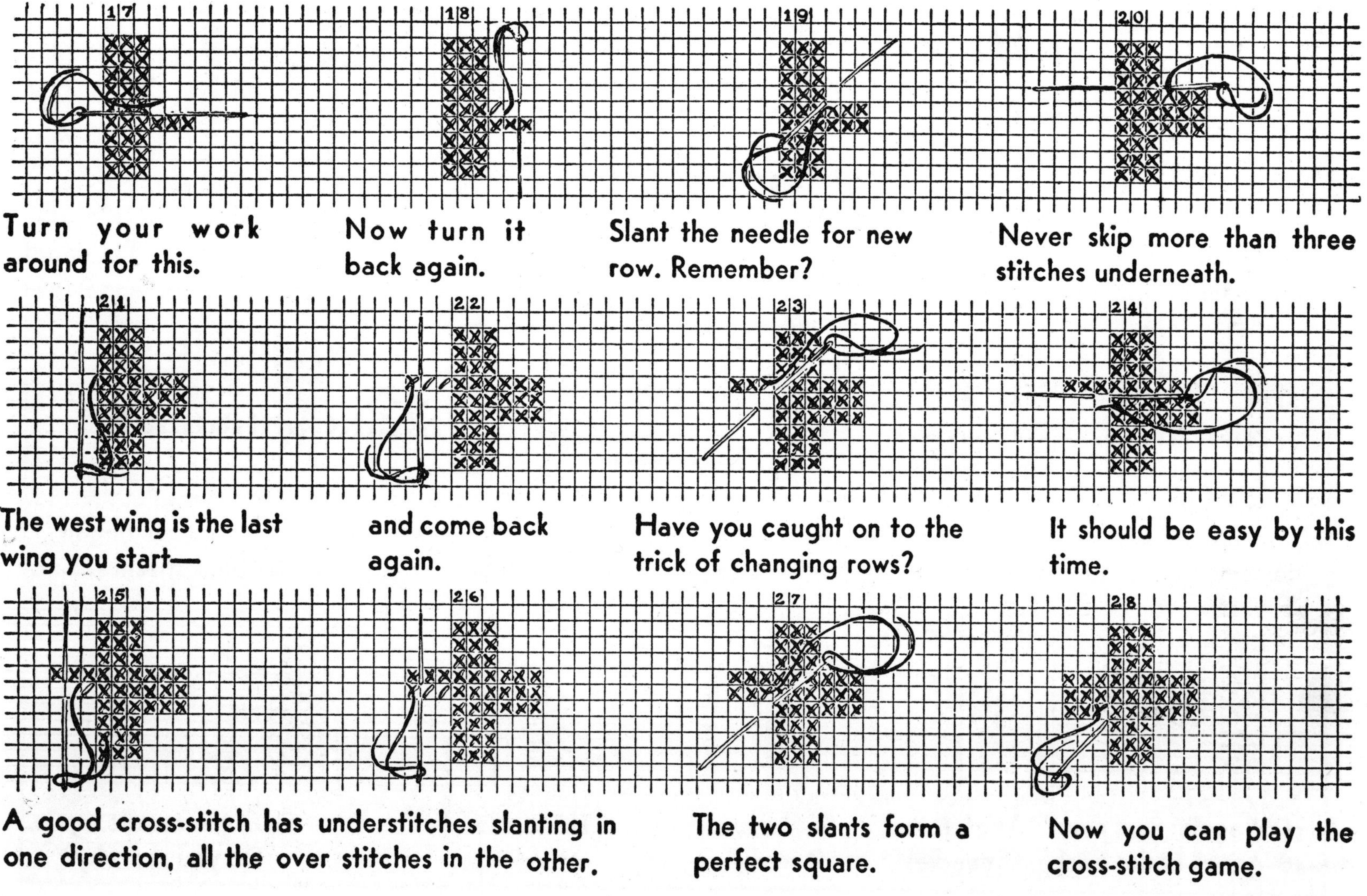


Turn your work around for this.

Now turn it back again.

Slant the needle for new row. Remember?

Never skip more than three stitches underneath.

The west wing is the last wing you start—

and come back again.

Have you caught on to the trick of changing rows?

It should be easy by this time.

A good cross-stitch has understitches slanting in one direction, all the over stitches in the other.

The two slants form a perfect square.

Now you can play the cross-stitch game.

# THESE WERE DESIGNED BY LITTLE GIRLS

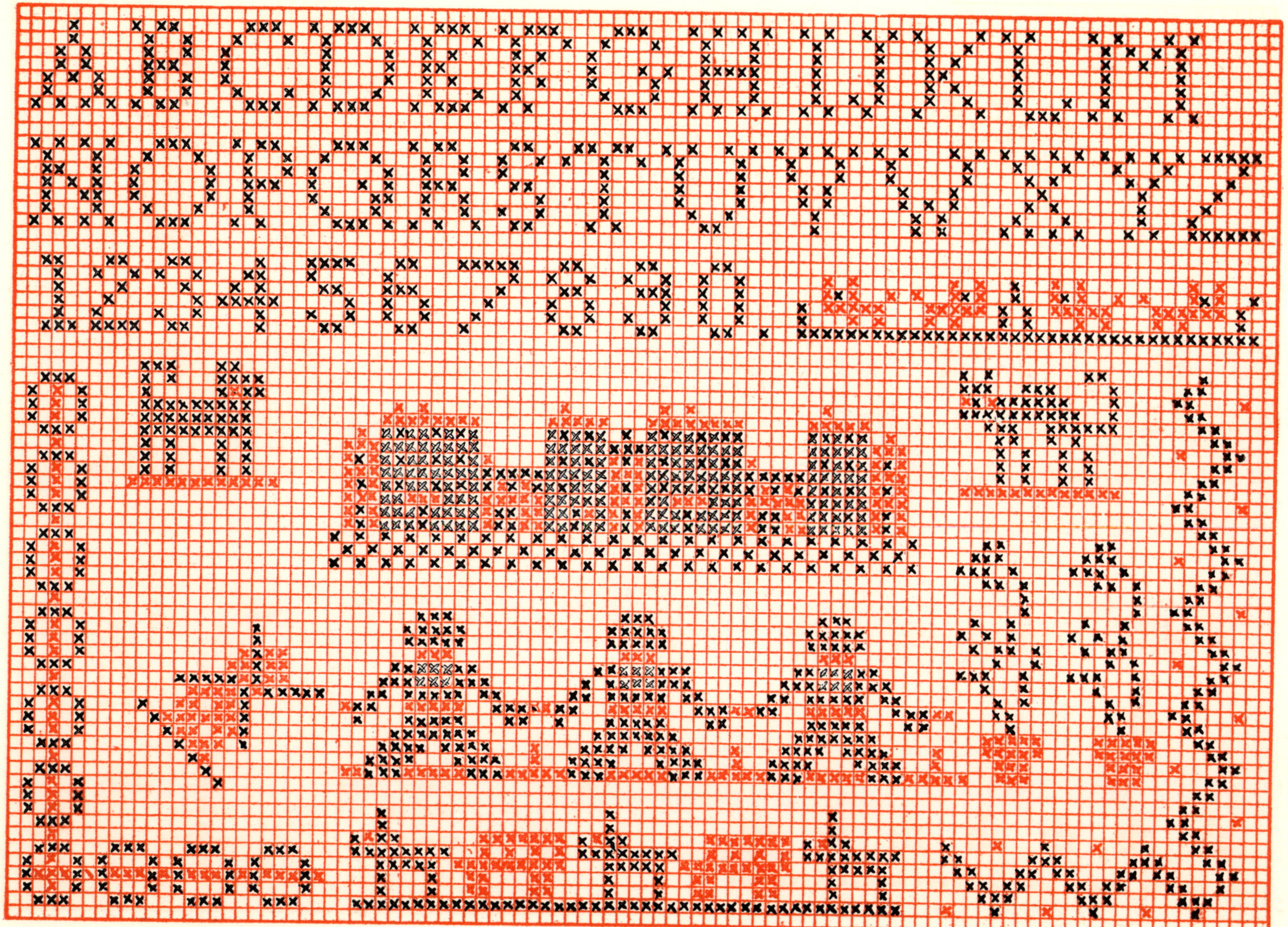

# DOES BASTING SAVE OR WASTE TIME?

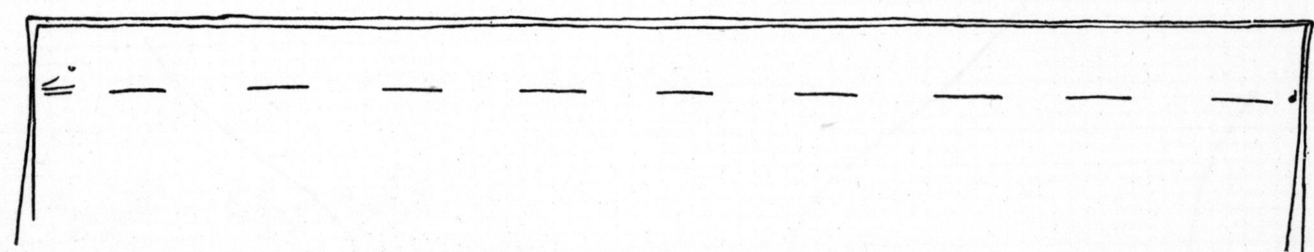

Basting is a large even running stitch, used to hold the work in place until it is sewed to stay. Start with a knot on the right side and end with two backstitches. To pull out, snip the backstitches through, and pull thread out by the knot. Always make your seam just a little below the basting.

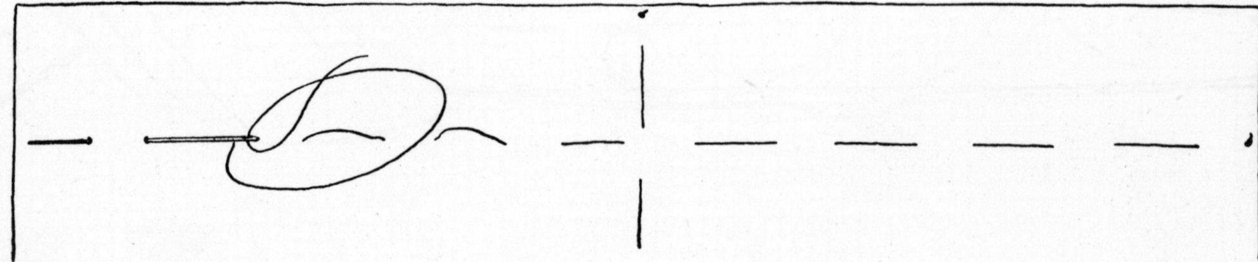

Uneven basting is often used for a guide-line on a single piece of material. (As, for instance, to mark the center where something will be embroidered.) Take larger stitches, make smaller spaces. A basting stitch in time saves a lot of ripping later!

# BASTE ON THE TABLE

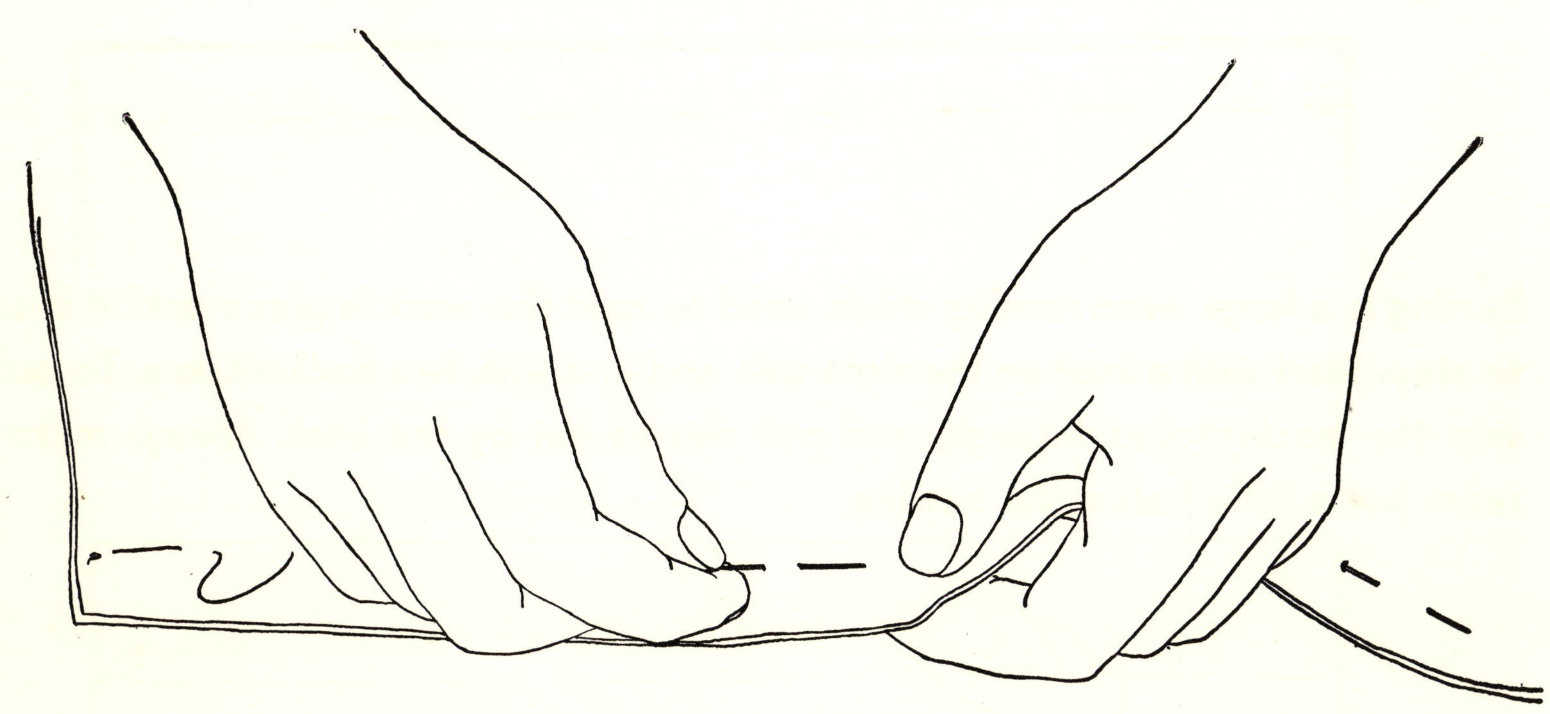

Long seams should be basted flat on the table. The edges then will not stretch or pucker. Baste a half inch in from the edge so material will not ravel. Be sure to stitch through both layers of cloth.

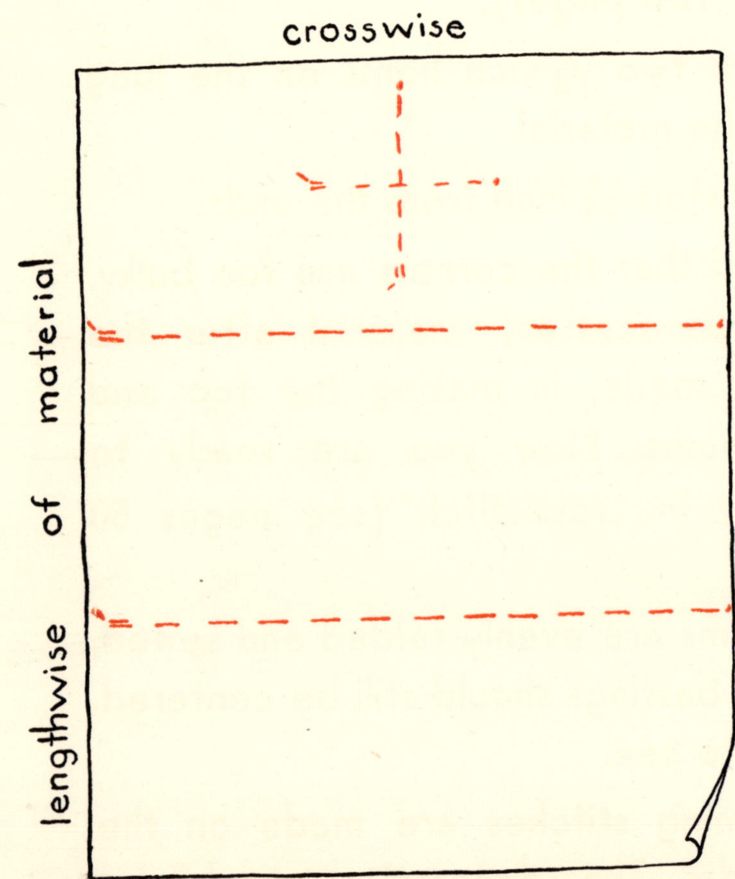


## MARKING OFF THE KIT

Cut the material 18 inches long and 11½ inches wide. Be sure you cut it straight on the grain. Fold it into three equal parts. Now you have three rectangles. Crease your folds and baste across (pages 20-54). Now mark the place where a decoration will be, by folding the top rectangle first crosswise, then lengthwise. Crease the folds. Baste a few stitches across the middle of the two creases to mark the place. This marks the center rows of your decorative design. If your cloth ravels fast do the markings after the edges are hemmed.

All bastings will be removed later.

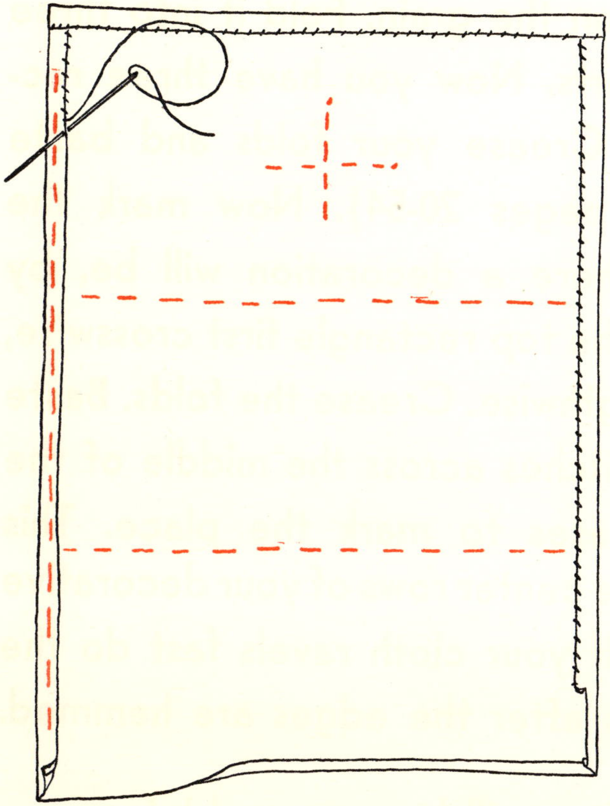

# MAKING THE KIT

Now you can start hemming the edges (see next two pages).

First make two ½-inch hems on the long sides of the material.

Start and stop ¾ inch from the ends.

If you find that the corners are too bulky, cut the unnecessary material after the crease is made, in making the top and bottom hems. Now you are ready to embroider in cross-stitch (see pages 50 and 51).

If your hems are evenly folded and sewed, the guide bastings should still be centered. Measure to see.

The hemming stitches are made on the wrong side. The decoration should be embroidered on the right side.

# MAKING A NARROW HEM

A hem is made by folding over the raw edge twice so it is hidden, and then sewing down this fold.

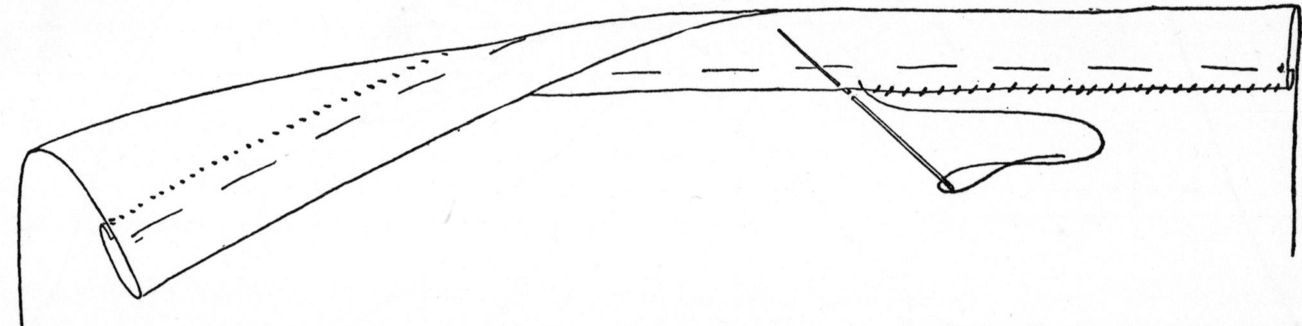

Baste hem near folded edge to keep fold in place.

To start: Slip knot under edge of fold. Take three threads of your material and on the same needle three threads of the folded edge. Keep needle slanted to the left. The stitches will have a slant on both sides.

If the stitches are too large, they will show on the right side. If too small, the weight of the hem will break the thread of the goods in washing.

# CREASING A HEM

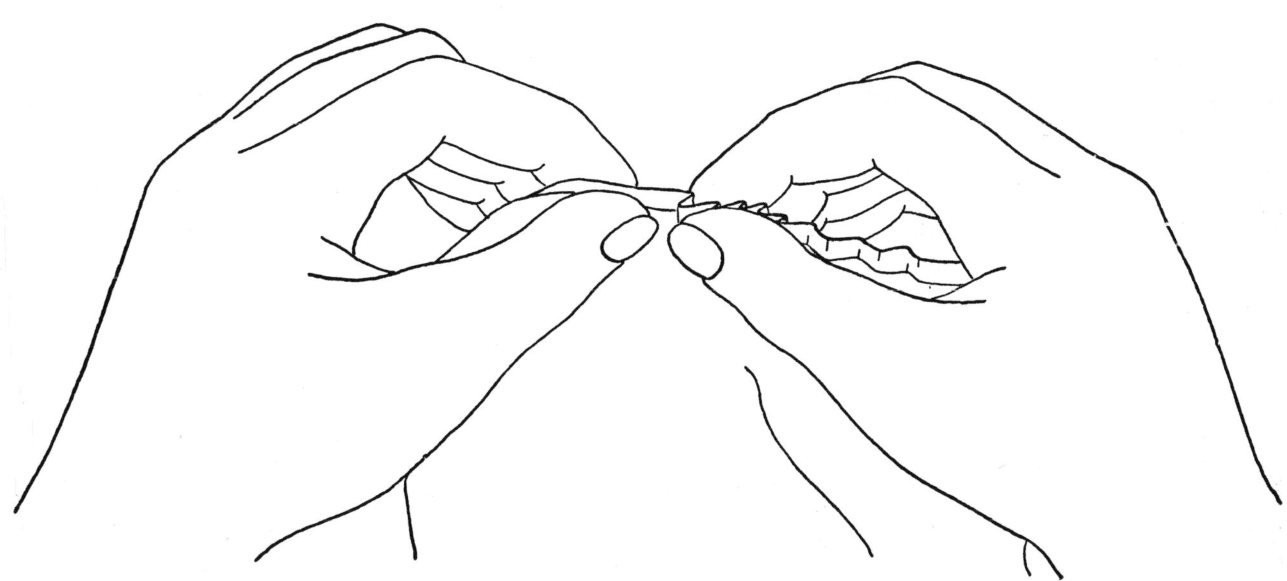

Creasing a hem helps to keep the folds in place until they are sewed. Make about three little pleats between two fingers, press with fingers, then let go. If material is wiry, like flannel, first fold has to be basted, then pressed into place with an iron. For very narrow hems in thin materials, fold over 1/8 inch to the wrong side and crease. Turn second fold enough to cover this first fold and crease. For heavier fabrics, fold 1/4 inch first and then whatever width you want your hem to be for the second. The evenness of the hems will depend on the neatness of your two folds. Watch that you do not stretch the material when you make a hem on the crosswise of the goods.

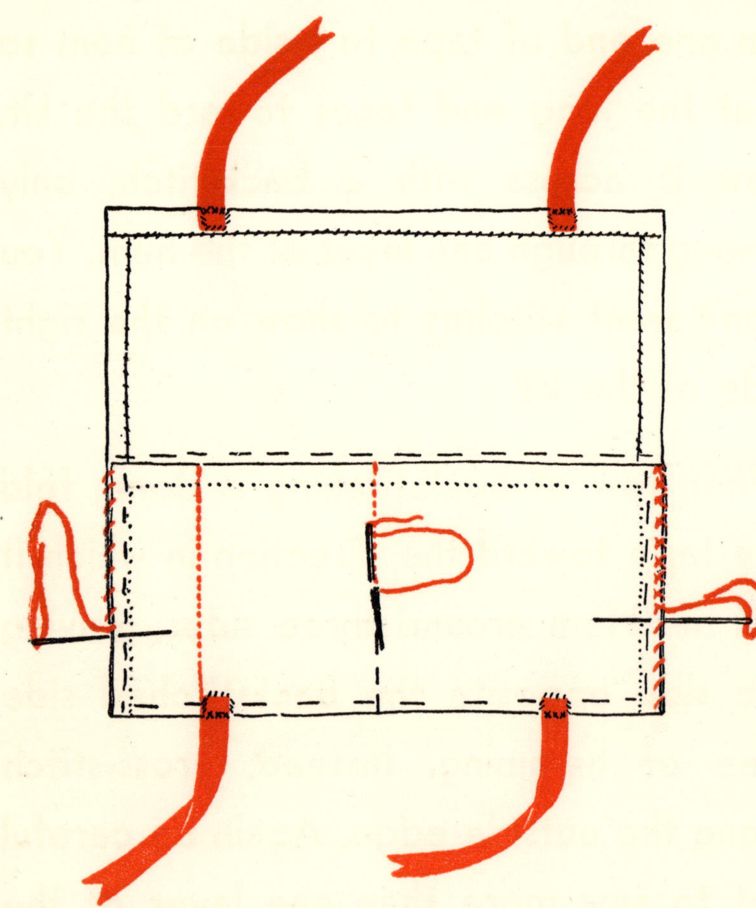

## FINISHING UP THE KIT

Put your beautifully hemmed and cross-stitched piece on the table, the wrong side facing you. Fold it so that the bottom hem falls on the upper basted line. Baste the two sides of the kit through the hems. Then, with the same red cotton that you used to make the decoration, start a double overcasting from the bottom corner (see page 36). Make your stitches the size of the cross-stitch you used in the center. Finish well before you cut the thread. Sew the other side the same way but start overcasting at the top of the pocket this time. Sew on tapes about 8 inches long (see next page). In sewing on the bottom ties, put your hand inside the pocket to make sure the stitching does not go through both sides of the pocket. If you wish to divide the pocket use backstitching through both layers. Baste for guide, so small pockets will be straight.

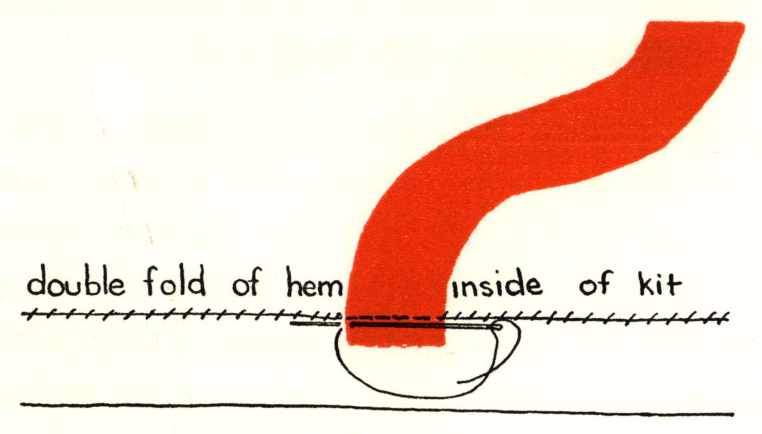


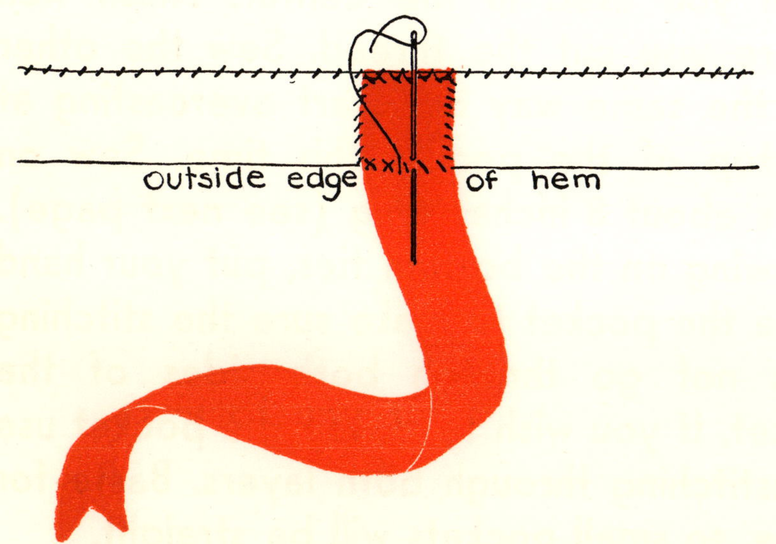


## HOW TO SEW TAPE ON TO STAY

Pin one end of tape to inside of hem so that the long end faces toward the kit. Sew it across with a backstitch, only sewing through one layer of the hem. You don't want stitches to show on the right side of the kit.

When row of backstitching is done, fold the tape toward the direction in which it will tie. Hem around three sides, leaving the side opposite the backstitched side free of hemming. Instead, cross-stitch along the outside edge. Again be careful not to sew more than one layer of the hem. Fasten end of thread by taking three small stitches one over the other.

## GIFT SUGGESTIONS

You can make any number of things with material hemmed around and a few cross-stitches. A glove case the size of the kit, with just a single pocket. Tie it with a grosgrain ribbon if your work deserves it.

Books that are used a great deal like cook books or a telephone directory, will last longer and look nicer. . . . You can make two pockets to slip the cover into.

A knitting-needle case will be a most useful present to your favorite aunt, who is bound to knit you a sweater in gratitude.

A handkerchief case, a stocking case, a sewing kit . . . just suggestions for you to work out. Make the size fit the object to go into it. Allow for the hems, so Love's Labor won't be lost.

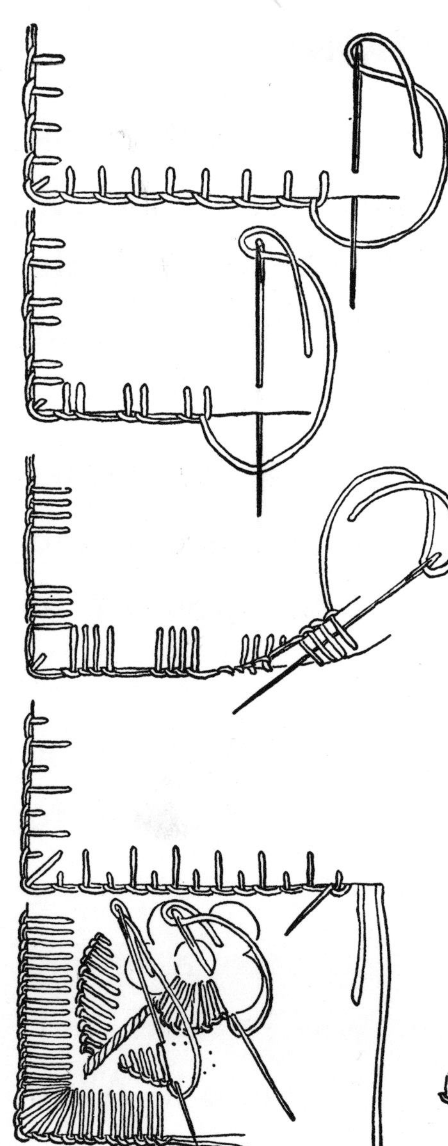

## THESE ARE ALL BLANKET STITCHES

The blanket stitch was first used on blankets to stop their edges from raveling. The cloth was too heavy to turn under and hem. Sometimes we use blanket stitches as decoration. Materials that are not too thick should be turned under. Basting will hold the edges in place if it is hard for you to keep them turned under evenly.

You can have fun changing the size and space of stitch to get different results.

To turn corners, put in two or more stitches in the same place. A tiny stitch (as shown at left) will also help to hold down the corner. To finish thread, turn over and pass under finished stitches, then cut off.

To start new thread, pass it under a few finished stitches and bring needle out on top through the last loop. It must catch the loop to look unbroken. If you do your stitches closely, using yarn, they make a lovely border. You can also use blanket stitch to make leaves and flowers.

This beginner started to grow, not sew, her blanket stitches.

# HOW TO HOLD BLANKET STITCHING

Start with a knot on the wrong side.
If you have a folded edge, hide the knot in the fold.

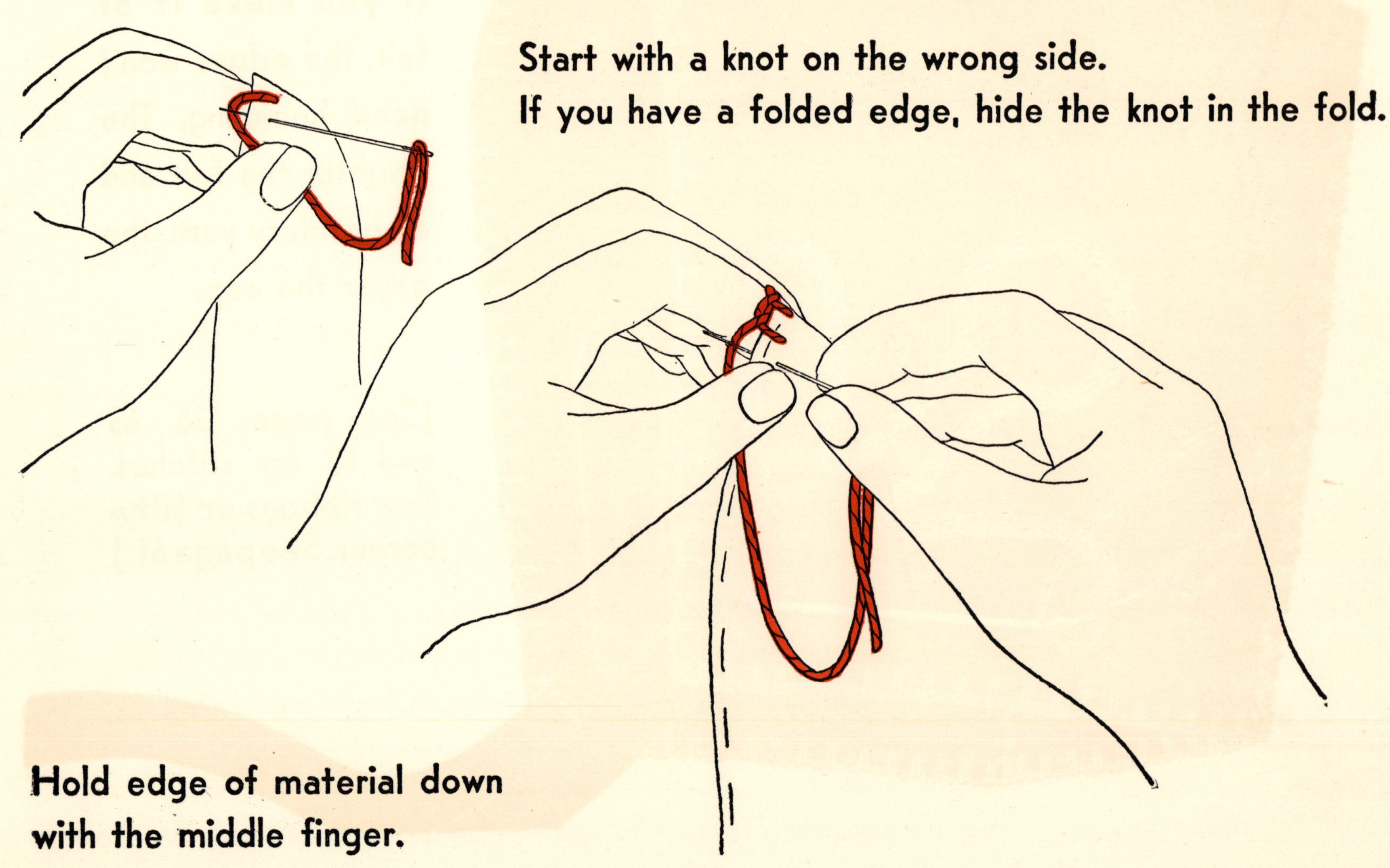

Hold edge of material down with the middle finger.

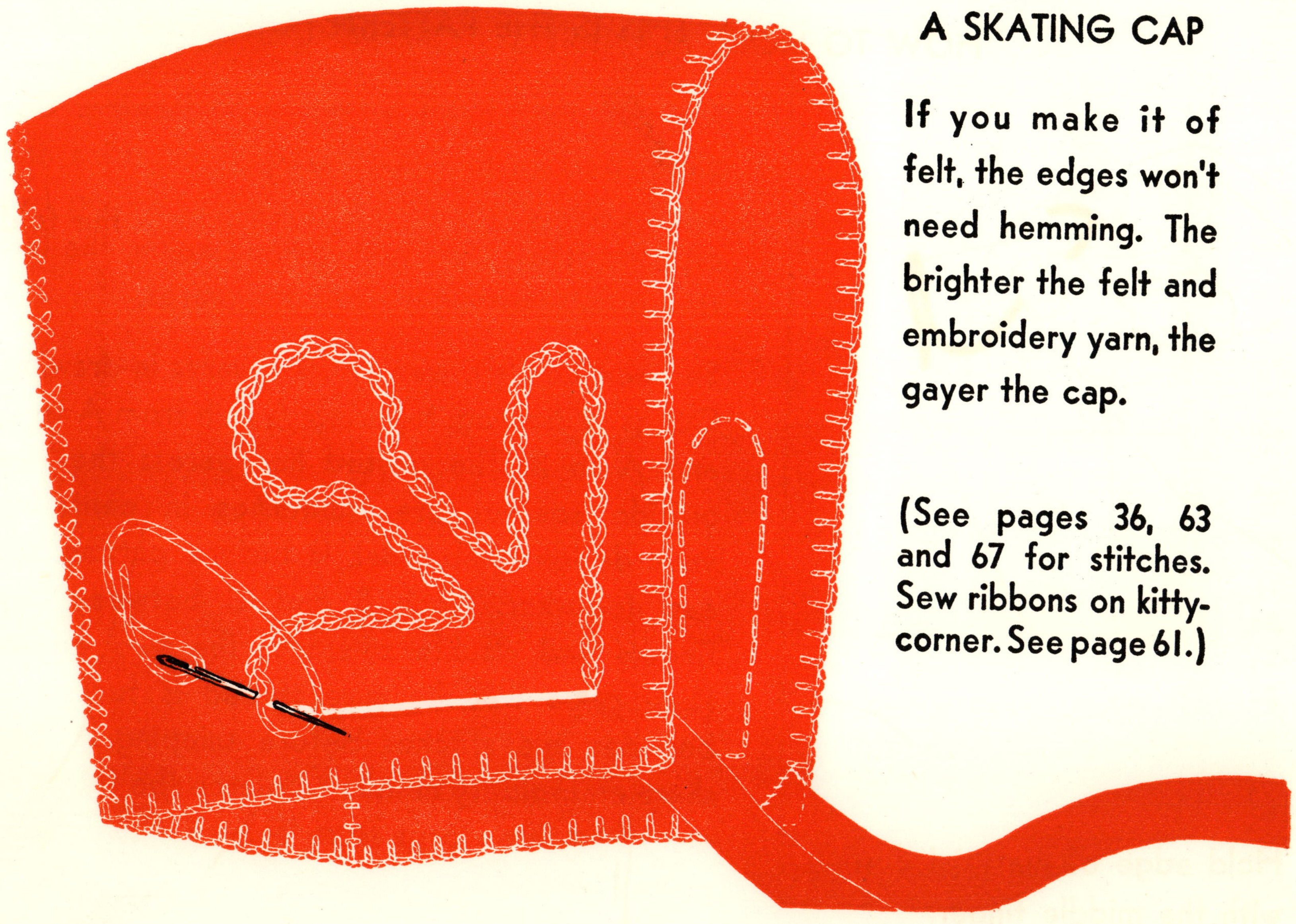

## A SKATING CAP

If you make it of felt, the edges won't need hemming. The brighter the felt and embroidery yarn, the gayer the cap.

(See pages 36, 63 and 67 for stitches. Sew ribbons on kitty-corner. See page 61.)

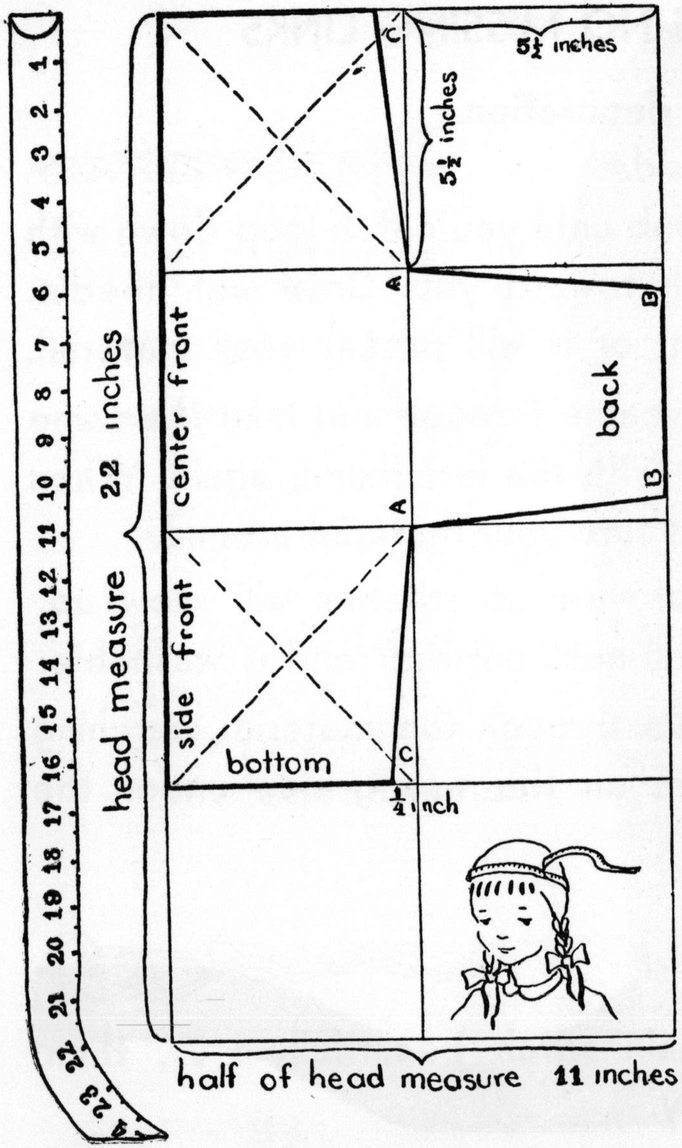

# THIS IS THE PATTERN FOR YOUR CAP

Measure your head as shown in drawing. Cut paper pattern the length of your headsize and half as wide. Fold paper crosswise, making two equal squares. Now fold it twice again, the last fold giving you eight perfect squares.

See how cap is drawn on six squares in drawing. Cut as in drawing, tapering 1/4 inch from A to C and A to B. The dotted line across the two outside squares are guidelines in centering your design. Embroider it before putting the cap together. Pinch B and C between two fingers and double overcast the two edges. (See page 36.) Be sure thread is tucked in between the stitches before snipping it. Use sharp embroidery needle to pierce the felt. You can make three caps from 1/3 yard of felt, as it comes very wide.

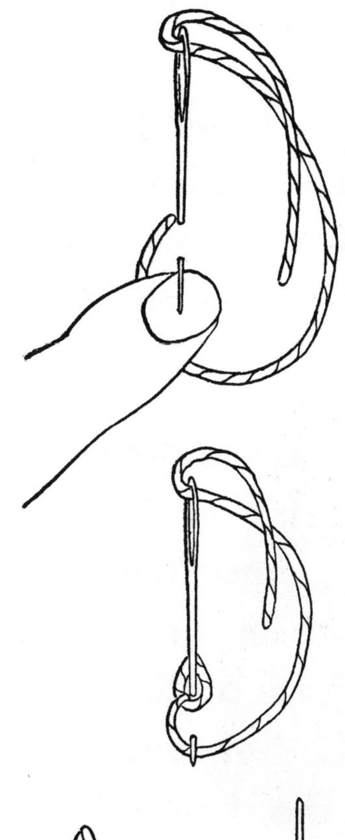

## THERE SHOULD BE NO MISSING LINKS

Chain stitch is a stitch used for decoration.

Start with a knot on the wrong side.

Hold thread down with left thumb until you catch loop down with next stitch. Take a small stitch toward you. Draw out needle. Never pull your stitch too tight or it will pucker your material.

Put needle back into hole it just came through and take the same size stitch, holding thread down with the left thumb again. When you come to curves and corners turn your material around.

Use a heavy crochet cotton or yarn so stitches will show up. "D. M. C. Embroidery Twist" will not "untwist" and is washable.

To end chain stitch, push needle through the material, catching down the last loop, and fasten on the wrong side under the finished stitches.

A ten-year-old started her chain stitch beautifully . . . then decided to finish the row quickly.

# THESE ARE BIRDS OF DIFFERENT FEATHERS

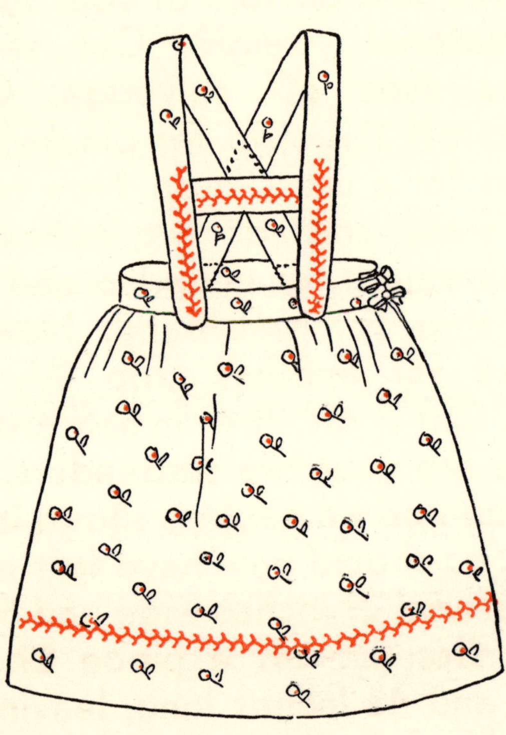

How about a skirt made by and for yourself? The one above is trimmed with simple featherstitch on the hem and suspenders. Featherstitch looks nice on printed, as well as plain cloth.

In this skirt you put the hand in the bird instead of the bird in the hand. They look best on a plain material. If you are ten years old, you'll need only 1½ yards of cloth, 36 inches wide.

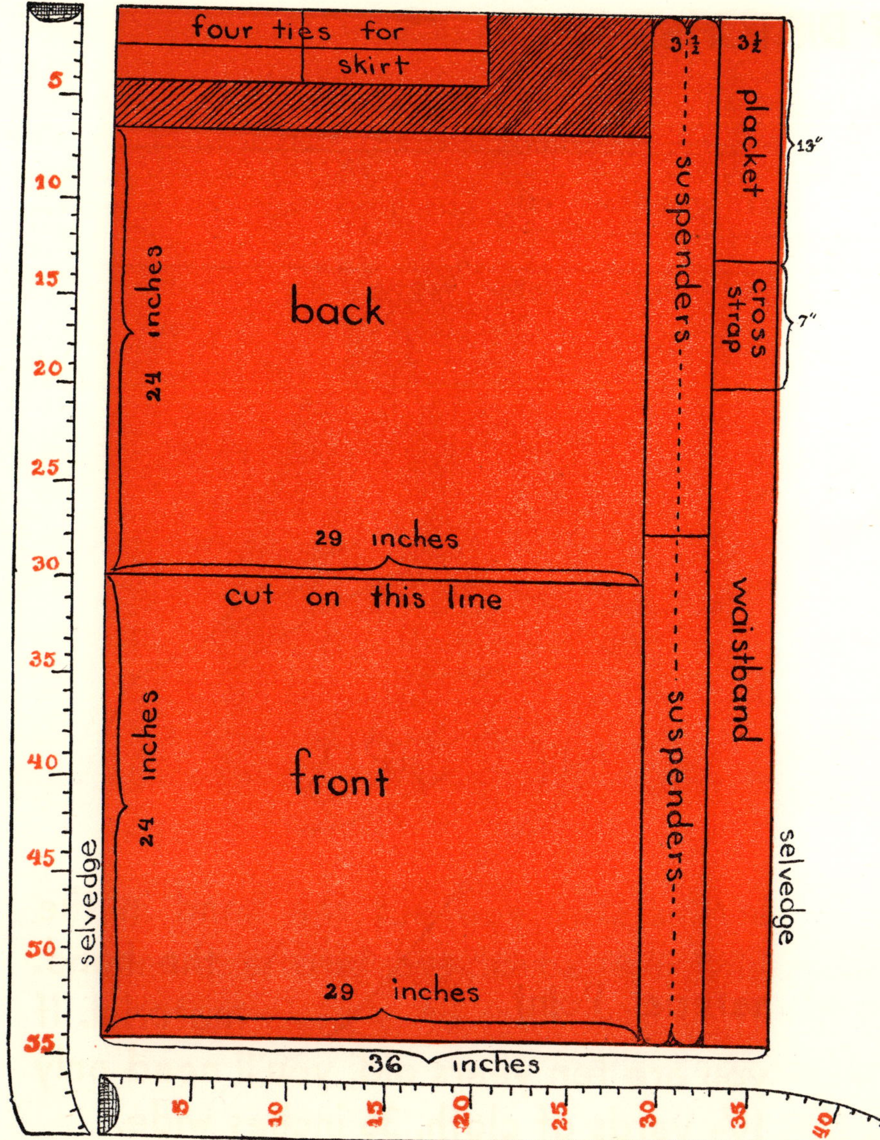


## CUTTING YOUR SKIRT (see page 3)

Cut top and bottom of your 1½ yards of material straight. Cut strip 3½ inches wide off selvedge. Cut 13 inches off this strip for placket, and 7 inches for a cross strap. Now measure your waist, and add two inches to the measurement for underlap and seams. Cut strip for waistband. Now draw thread for another strip 3½ inches wide. Cut it off; then in half crosswise. These are your two suspenders. Round off one end on each as shown in drawing. You should now have left a piece of material 29 inches wide and 54 long. From this cut off a piece 29 inches wide and 48 inches long, leaving only 6 inches of the original piece, 29 inches wide. Out of this you will cut your skirt-ties. The large piece must be cut in two to make the front and back of your skirt. Each should measure 24 inches long by 29 wide.

# TO CUT NOTCHES

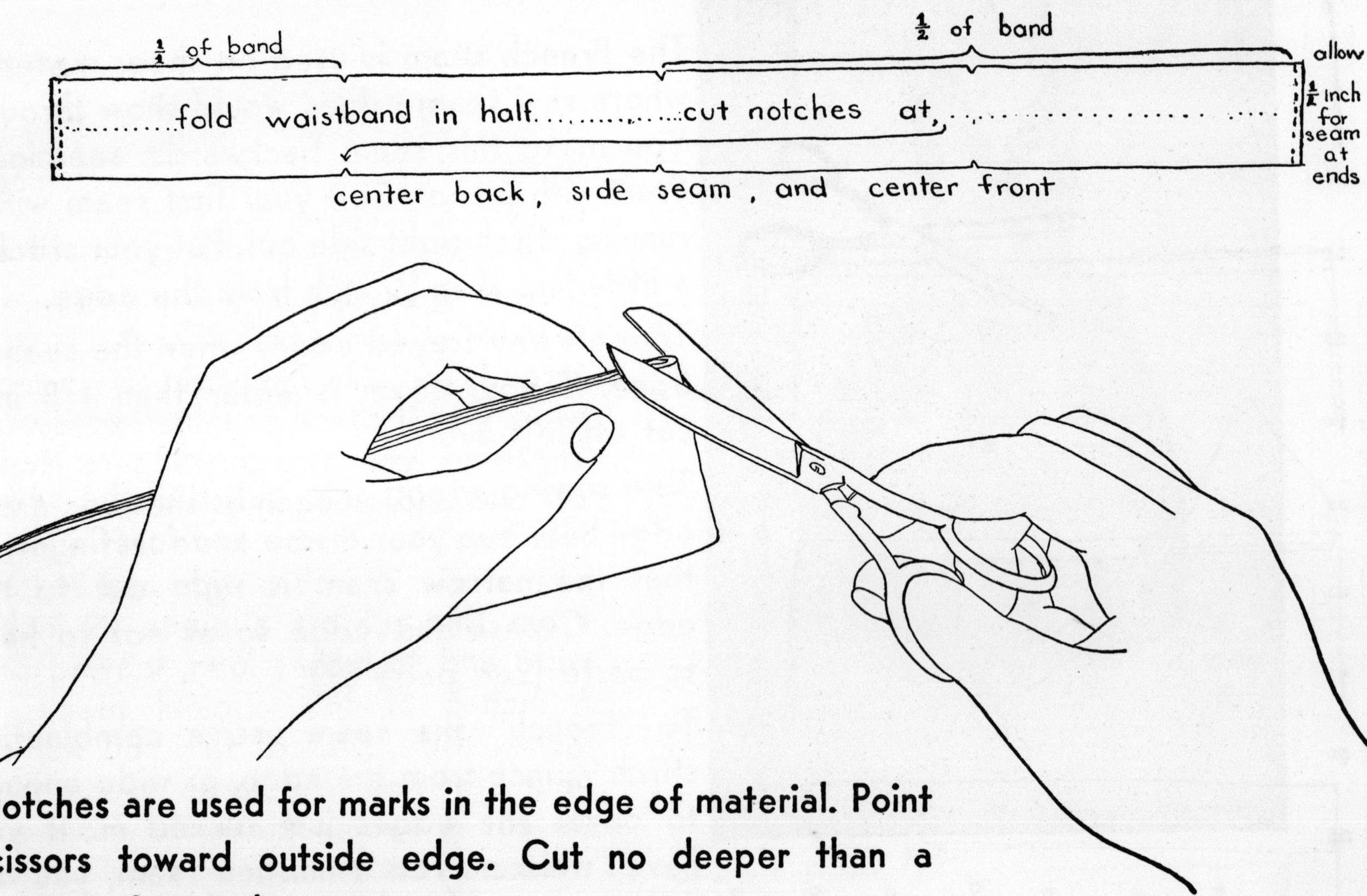


**Notches are used for marks in the edge of material. Point scissors toward outside edge. Cut no deeper than a quarter of an inch.**

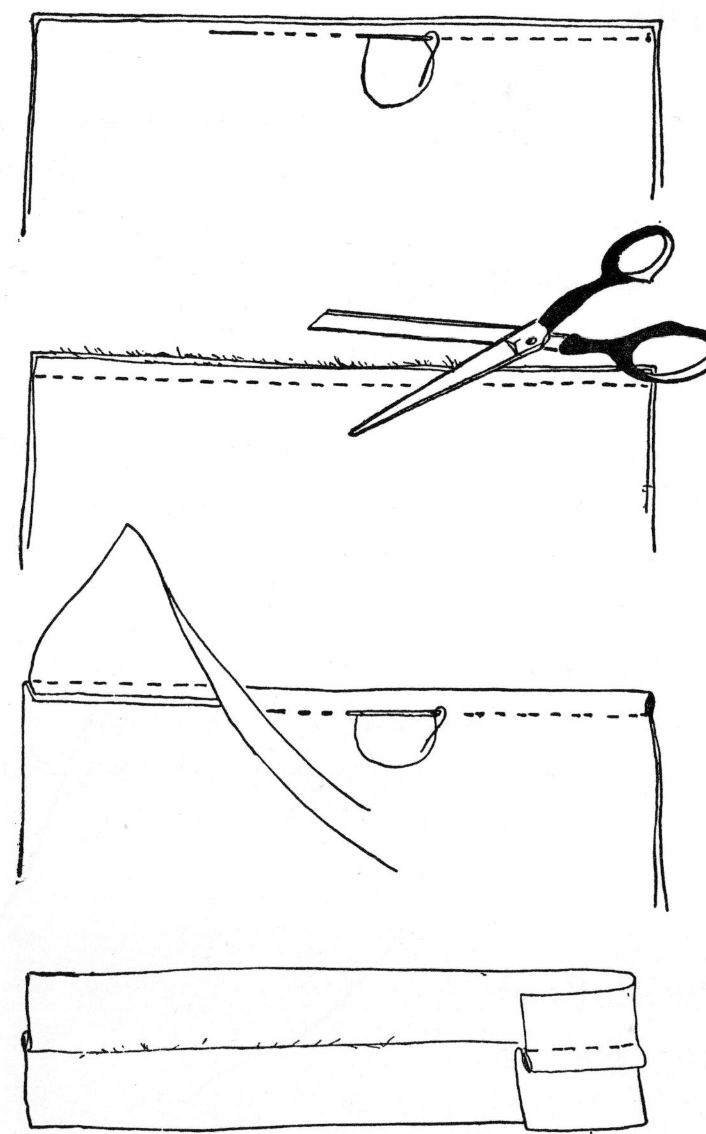

## THE FRENCH SEAM

The French seam is used on sheer materials where raw seam edges would show through. You make this seam backwards, seemingly. Start with a knot. Sew your first seam with a running stitch right side out. Put your stitches a little less than 1/4 inch from the edge.

Trim off any frayed edges when the seam is done. If your seam is wider than 1/8 inch cut off left-over.

Turn sewing wrong side out. Roll the sewed edge between your thumb and forefinger, so that the narrow seam is right out to the edge. Crease this edge so as not to have to baste (see page 59).

To "French" the seam use a combination stitch 1/4 inch from the edge, or wide enough to cover the edges just tucked in. If you have "whiskers" on a finished seam, you did not trim frayed edges close enough.

# PUTTING THE SKIRT TOGETHER

selvedge

Lay the back and front of your skirt together, right side out on the table, with selvedges on the left side. Put a notch (page 70) in the right side through both layers 6 inches from the top. Mark front center of the skirt at the top and bottom with notches.

Mark center back at the top only. To mark center front for putting on pockets evenly, baste between the two notches in the top and bottom of the skirt.

Make a plain seam on the side of the selvedge 1/2 inch deep. Use a combination stitch. Make a French seam (a plain seam if cloth is heavy) on the other side up to the notches.

Put in a continuous placket (see opposite page). Make two or three rows of gathering stitches (see page 74) around top 3/8 inch from the edge. Gather the skirt to fit waistband (see page 75). Then put in the hem (see pages 76-77).

# MAKING A PLACKET

Plackets are the openings on dresses or skirts so you can get them on. A continuous placket is the strongest. This folded piece of cloth continues on both sides of the opening.

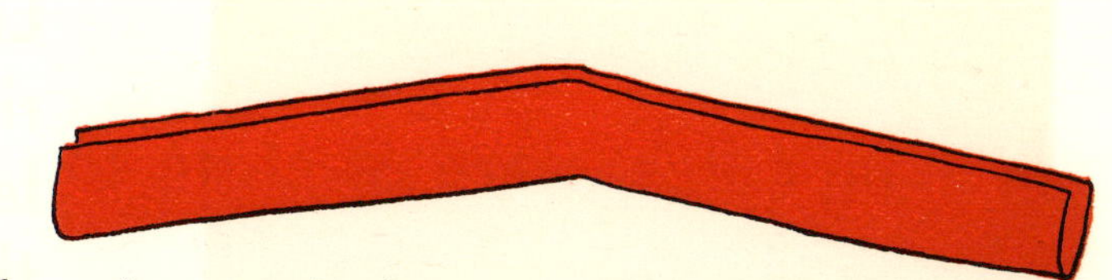

1. Baste one long edge of the strip along both edges of the opening. Use running stitch starting ¼ inch at the top of the placket and narrowing to 1/8 inch from the edge at the lower end. Take a few backstitches at the turn for extra strength.
2. Turn skirt wrong side out. The other long edge is now turned under and hemmed close to the first seam.
3. The placket will be hidden when closed. No stitch or seam will show on the front side of the placket, because it is turned under.

The side of the placket sewed to the back of the skirt is the underlap.

1

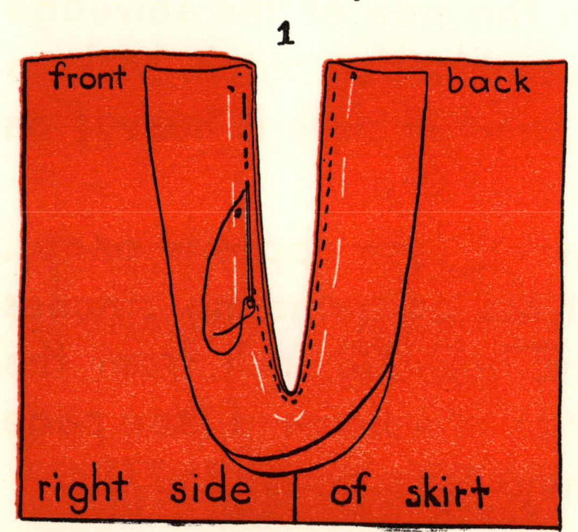


2

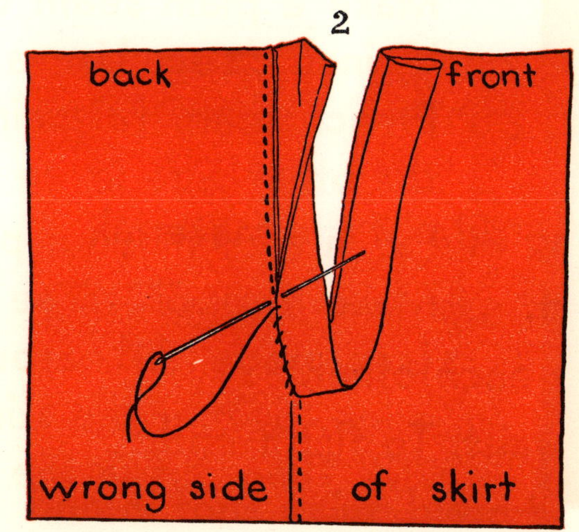


3

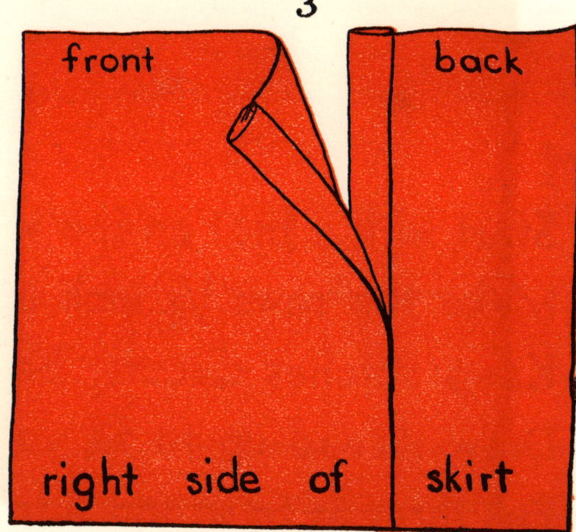

# HERE WE GO A-GATHERING

Gathering stitches are as close together as running stitches, but the stitches on the right side are twice as long. Use double thread. For your skirt gathers you will need it one yard long.

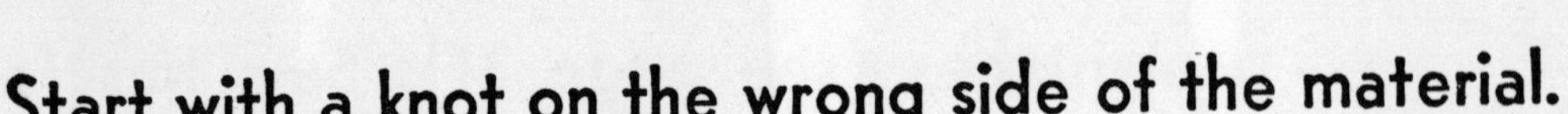

Start with a knot on the wrong side of the material.
Make the rows 1/4 inch apart.
Keep stitches directly below each other.
Draw thread up to fit your waist. To finish ends:
Pull threads to wrong side and braid, tying knot in end, or finish like running stitches.

# PUTTING ON A BAND

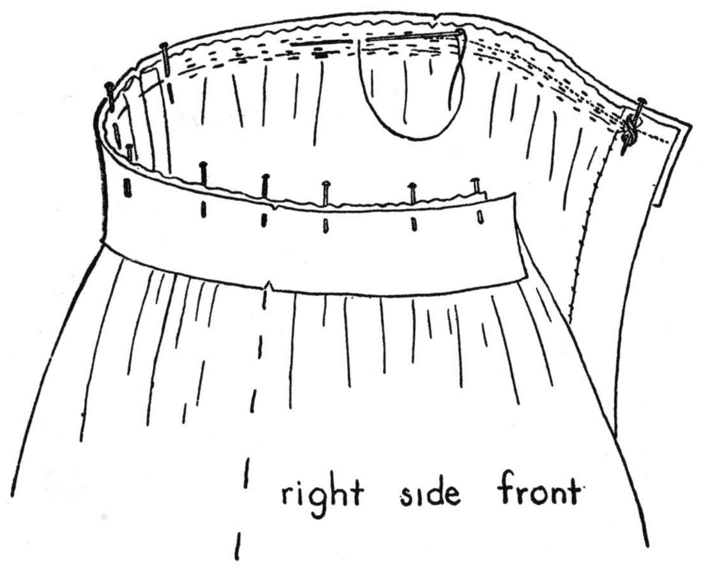


Place center of band on side seam of skirt and pin it. The other notches you marked on your skirt center (back and front) can now be pinned to the two notches between center and the end of the band. The two ends stick out a half inch beyond the plackets for the seam. Draw up your gathering threads until they are the same length as the waistband. Fasten the thread around the pin as you tie a kite in a figure 8.

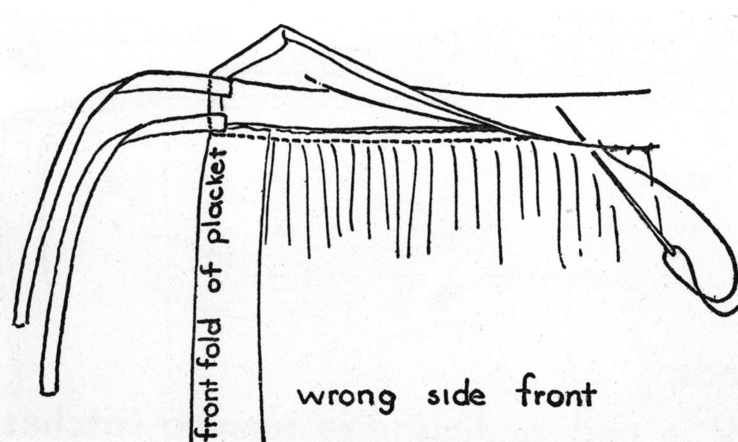


Turn skirt inside out to baste on band with backstitches (see page 31). Sew ties for skirt on front edge with backstitches before the seam is turned in. After the band and skirt are sewed together, hem the band down. Now you can do the bottom hem.

# MAKING WIDE HEM WITH A GAUGE

Before you put the bottom hem in the skirt, you have to try it on. See that it is even all around. Turn up the hem with pins first to be sure that the length you decide on is right. Baste all around the bottom edge. Try on again to make sure. It is better to leave this type of skirt too long than too short. For the first fold, crease ¼ inch (see page 59). You can only get an even hem if both folds are even.

Make a gauge out of an inch-wide cardboard. Measure the width of the hem-to-be after the first fold is made. If hem is to be 1½ inches wide, measure 1½ inches down from the top of the cardboard. Make a line ¼ of an inch to the left. Measure ⅜ of an inch down. Connect the two points. Cut out triangle and use straight line for marking hem.

# POSITION FOR HEMMING

In sewing hems, you must feel the folded edge between your fingers. Your thumb is holding down the fold. The needle slants toward the left shoulder.

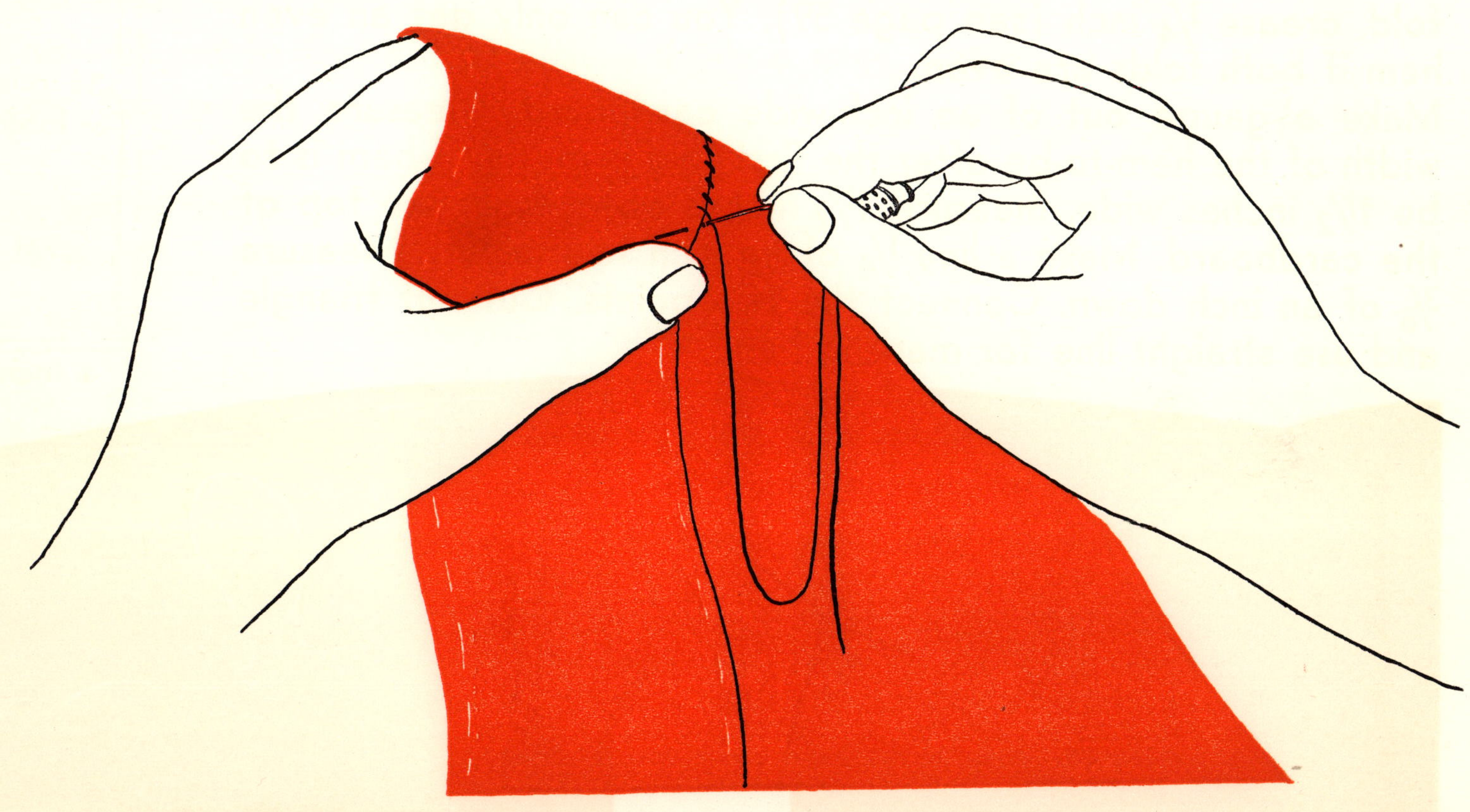

# FEATHER STITCHING AS NEAT AS A FEATHER

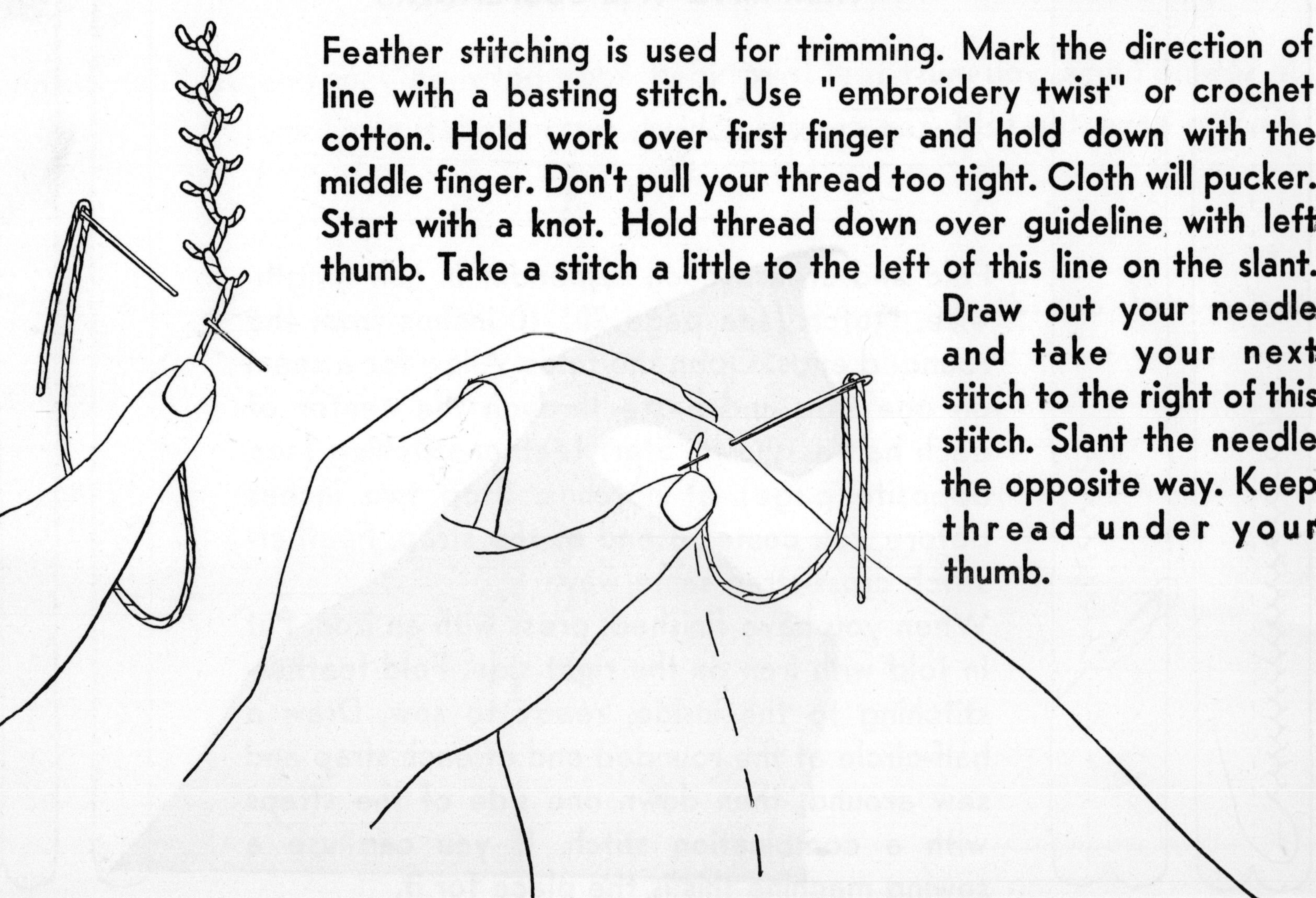

Feather stitching is used for trimming. Mark the direction of line with a basting stitch. Use "embroidery twist" or crochet cotton. Hold work over first finger and hold down with the middle finger. Don't pull your thread too tight. Cloth will pucker. Start with a knot. Hold thread down over guideline with left thumb. Take a stitch a little to the left of this line on the slant. Draw out your needle and take your next stitch to the right of this stitch. Slant the needle the opposite way. Keep thread under your thumb.

# TRIMMING THE SUSPENDERS

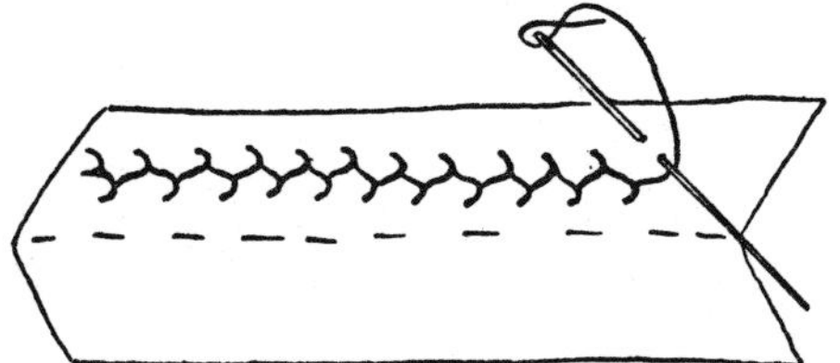

Fold and crease each suspender in half lengthwise. Notch (see page 70) 10 inches from the rounded ends. Open the folds. Allow for a seam on one side and baste through the center of each half as shown. Start feather stitching (see opposite page) at notches. Stop two inches before you come to end of the strap. Featherstitch cross-strap same way.

When you have finished, press with an iron. Put in fold with iron on the right side. Fold featherstitching to the inside, ready to sew. Draw a half-circle at the rounded end of each strap and sew around, then down one side of the straps with a combination stitch. If you can use a sewing machine this is the place for it.

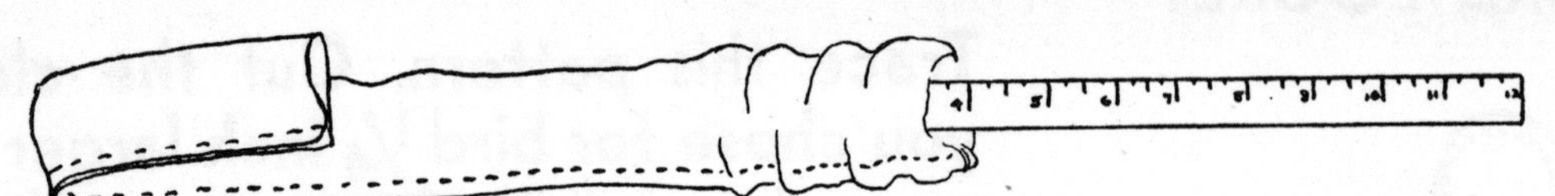

## FINISHING UP

Turn the suspenders inside out by pushing end of ruler against rounded tip of strap. Push ruler slowly. Meanwhile using left hand to push cloth onto ruler. When you make ties for the waist, turn them right side out with a safety pin. Mark the back of the suspenders 6 inches above the curved end with a pin. Lay sewed edge of crossbar against strap and pin crossbar on. Suspenders should slant out a bit from the waist to the shoulder. Now turn the suspenders to the right side, and change the pins to the right side, so they won't prick you.

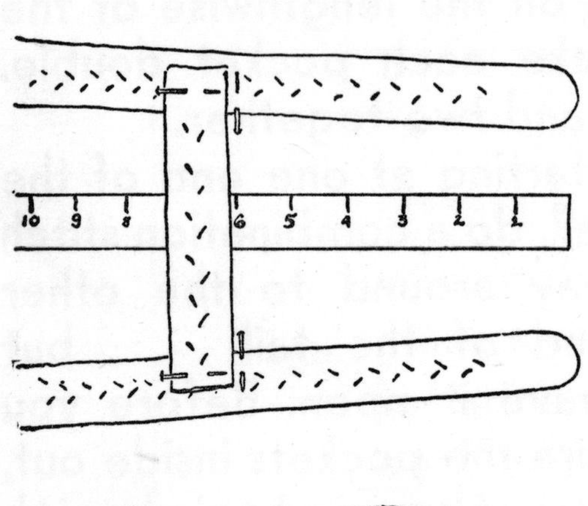

Remove other pins and try on. Pin to waistband in front, cross in back and pin . . . or ask your mother to do it for you. Adjust to right length and width at shoulders so the suspenders won't ride off. Finish the featherstitching by taking the stitches through the waistband, too. Turn to the wrong side again. Hem the crossbar, the crossing in the back, and the suspenders to the waistband in the back. Sew as you would tape. Sew the two ties on the opposite side of the waist.

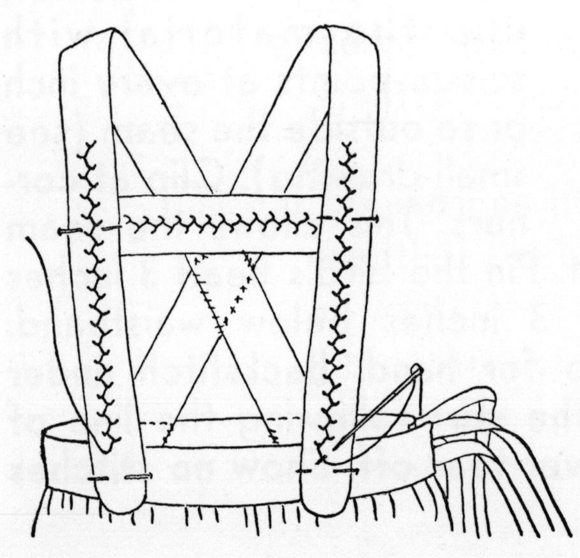

## HAND-IN-BIRD POCKET

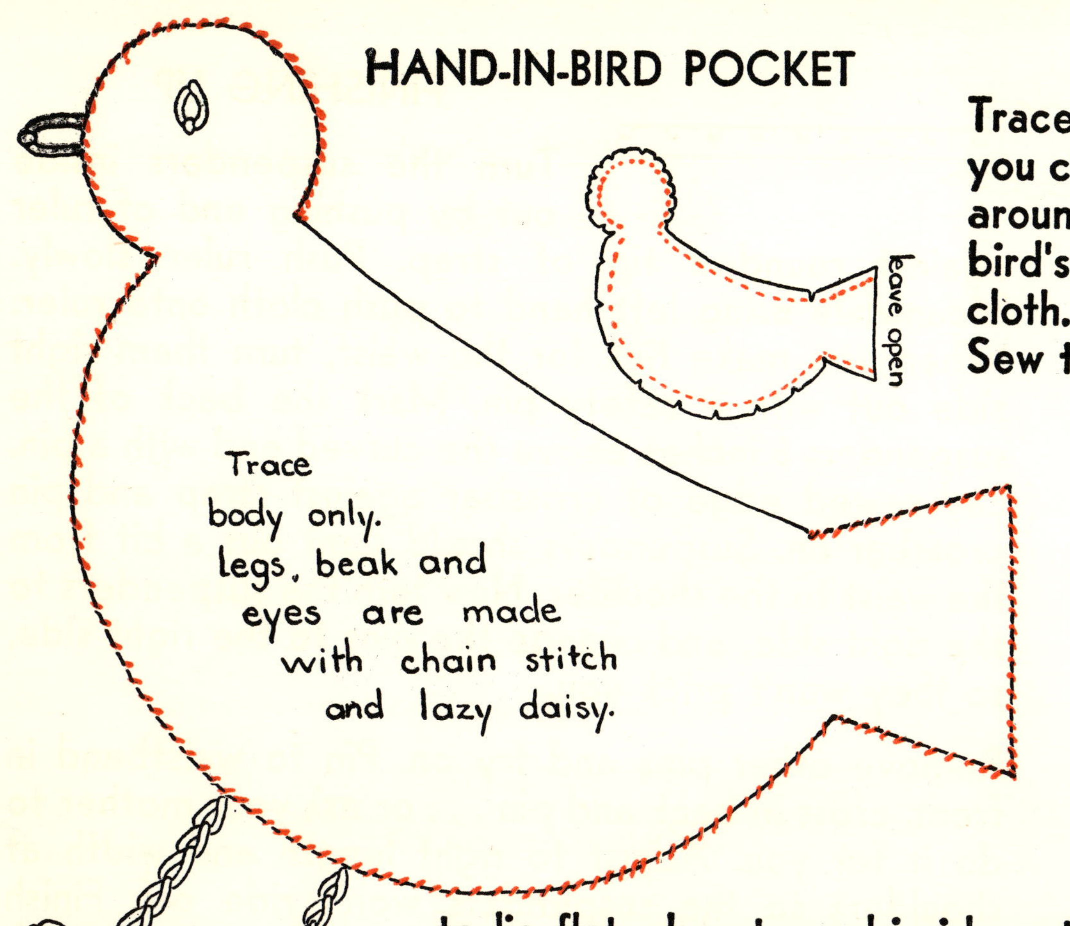


Trace this pattern. Cut the cloth you chose for bird 1/4 inch larger all around to allow for seams. Place bird's tail on the lengthwise of the cloth. Make each pocket double. Sew two and two together.

Starting at one end of the tail, do a combination stitch way around to the other end of the tail . . . but leave it open. Before you turn the pockets inside out, clip the material with scissor-points at every inch or so outside the seam (see small drawing). Clip at corners. This allows the seam to lie flat when turned inside out. Pin the bird's head 3 inches from the center of skirt, and 3 inches below waistband. Appliqué around, leaving space for hand. Backstitch under the bird on the wrong side of the skirt following the line of appliqué so your pockets will never tear off. Show no stitches on right side.

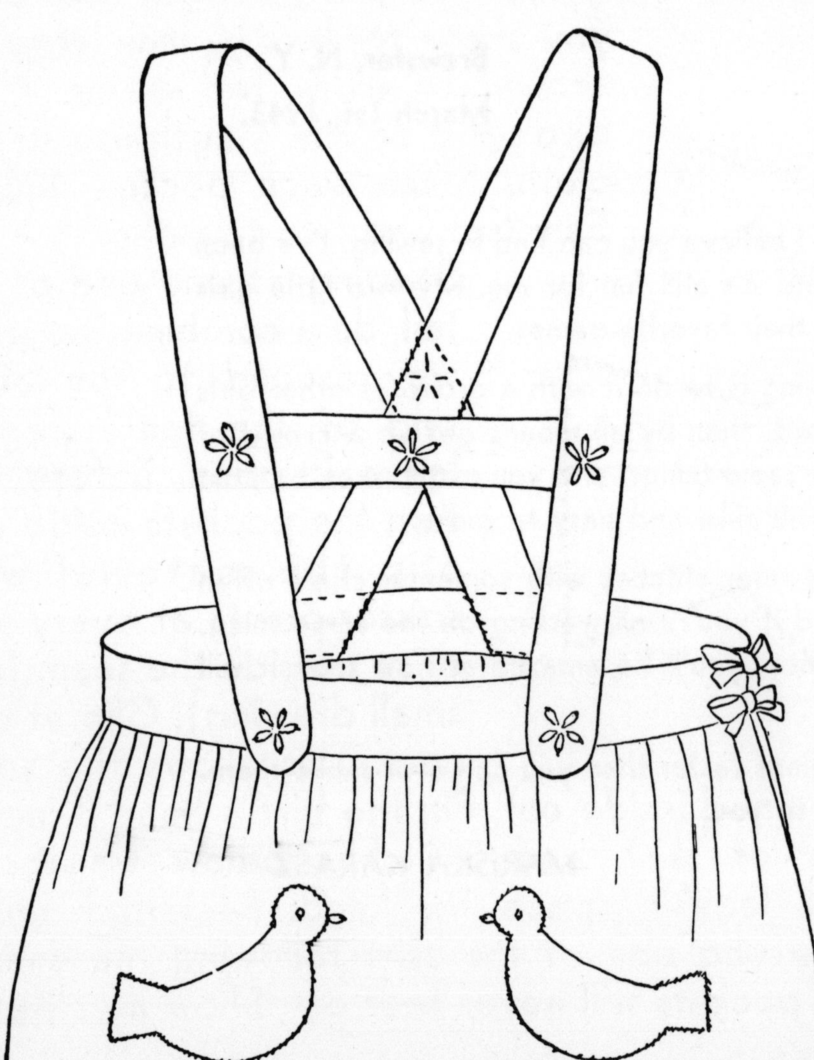

## LAZY DAISY

This stitch is a single chain stitch (see page 40).

Mark daisy's petals with dots in chalk.

Make each loop starting at the same center.

Make petals opposite each other.

Stitch through all layers of cloth.

Catch the loop down after each petal. Finish in center.

Brewster, N. Y.
March 1st, 1943.

Dear girls:

I'd like to tell you about the fun I believe you can find in sewing. I've been at it for a good many years, and it's still fun for me. My two little girls are doing it now, and it's one of their favorite games.

The best way to enjoy your sewing is to do it with a group of other girls your own age. If three is a crowd, then by all means get up a crowd of three. Then you can all make the same things, and you might even be able to make club uniforms that are all alike and easy to make.

Besides, being able to compare your stitches with someone else's often helps you to improve them. And if you're all working on the same thing, like a patchwork quilt, for instance, you'll be amazed at how soon it will be finished.

You will get ideas for making things faster than you can ever make them. So go to it . . . and good luck to you.

MARISKA KARASZ